Ancient Peoples and Places

EARLY CHRISTIAN
IRELAND

General Editor

DR GLYN DANIEL

ABOUT THE AUTHORS

Máire de Paor joined the Department of Archaeology, University College, Dublin in 1947 as assistant to the late Professor Ó Ríordáin. With him she excavated at Lough Gur and Tara. In 1954 she obtained her Ph.D. mainly for research on tenth-century metalworking. She has done special research into the Viking period in Ireland, has travelled extensively abroad and lectures and broadcasts on archaeological subjects. Her husband Liam, who is a lecturer in History at University College, Dublin, started his career as an architect and spent some years in the National Monuments Branch of the Irish Office of Public Works. Subsequently he studied Archaeology and Early Irish History and took his M.A. mainly for work in Irish Romanesque art. He has assisted on excavations in Ireland, Germany, Denmark, Norway and Portugal and has supervised excavations of medieval sites in Ireland.

Ancient Peoples and Places

EARLY CHRISTIAN IRELAND

Máire and Liam de Paor

76 PHOTOGRAPHS
31 LINE DRAWINGS
AND 5 MAPS

THAMES AND HUDSON

Ancient Peoples and Places

GENERAL EDITOR: GLYN DANIEL

To the memory of Seán P. Ó Ríordáin

© 1958 THAMES AND HUDSON LTD, LONDON

*Revised edition 1964
First paperback edition 1978
Originally published in the United States of America
in 1958 by Frederick A. Praeger, Inc.*

Library of Congress Catalog card number: 77-92265

Printed in Great Britain

CONTENTS

ILLUSTRATIONS

Note on this Edition

SINCE 1958, WHEN *Early Christian Ireland* was first published, research has proceeded both in archaeology and in history, and there have been some discoveries of significance. In particular, the excavations conducted in Dublin since 1962 by the National Museum of Ireland (chiefly under the direction of Mr Breandán Ó Ríordáin) have considerably changed our picture of Ireland in the Viking period. Some work has also been done at other town sites – Cork, Limerick and Wexford. The wealth of material recovered from Dublin shows that the city was of very considerable importance in the eleventh century as a trade and manufacturing centre. Work in metal, bone, wood and other materials, of very high quality, was produced there, and it is plain that this work had a widespread influence in Ireland. The dominance of Scandinavian art-styles in Ireland in the late eleventh and twelfth centuries is now much more understandable.

Historical research has modified our view of developments in Irish society. It now seems clear that many of the major monasteries had already begun to assume the character of towns independently of Viking settlement. The description of pre-Norman Irish society as essentially rural needs qualification. Monastic cities were probably not important trading centres but they had other town-like qualities and they were important centres of population, enjoying certain immunities and accumulating some negotiable wealth.

Some important works published since 1958 should be mentioned: L. Bieler, *Ireland: Harbinger of the Middle Ages*; M. Dillon and N. K. Chadwick, *The Celtic Realms*; I. Henderson, *The Picts*; F. Henry, *Irish Art* (3 vols); F. J. Byrne, *Irish Kings and High Kings*; K. Hughes, *The Church in Early Irish Society*; E. R. Norman and J. K. St Joseph, *The Early Development of Irish Society*; A. C. Thomas, *The Early Christian Archaeology of North Britain*.

Dublin *October 1977*

Finibus occiduis describitur optima tellus
  nomine et antiquis Scottia scripta libris.
dives opum, argenti, gemmarum, vestis et auri,
  commoda corporibus, aere, putri solo.
melle fluit pulchris et lacte Scottia campis,
  vestibus atque armis, frugibus, arte, viris.

       St Donatus, Bishop of Fiesole, c. A.D. *829–76*

Foreword

AN ADEQUATE ACCOUNT of the life and culture of Early Christian Ireland must be supported by all the available evidence, literary, historical, and archaeological, but since we are both archaeologists, writing ror what is primarily an archaeological series, we have tried to present an account that places the emphasis on the material manifestations of early Irish culture. In drawing freely on the literary evidence we have made use almost exclusively of edited and published sources, and on the whole we have relied upon the authority of scholars who are expert in the difficult linguistic and palaeographical sciences which share with archaeology the task of interpreting the early history of Ireland in the Christian era. In the field of archaeology we must acknowledge the debt which all students of this period owe especially to the scholars whose works are listed in the general section of our bibliography, and would particularly refer the reader to Dr Françoise Henry's *Irish Art* and *La sculpture irlandaise . . .*, Dr H. G. Leask's *Irish Churches and Monastic Buildings* and Dr Raftery's chapters in Vol. 2 of *Christian Art in Ancient Ireland*. We have occasionally departed from the views of these authorities, and must apologize for being unable, through lack of space, to offer detailed arguments for these divergencies.

In the spelling of proper names we have not attempted to be consistent but where a well-established anglicized form (such as Brian Boru) exists, we have used it; otherwise the forms occurring in contemporary or near-contemporary documents are used. Place-names which have survived in use into modern times are given in their anglicized forms as listed in the *Index of the Townlands, Baronies, and Parishes of Ireland*; otherwise they, too, are given in the old spelling.

We are especially grateful to Professor David Greene, who read the text before publication, advised us on our use of the early literature, and kindly supplied the new translation of a passage from the law-tract known as the *Crith Gablach* which appears on p. 78. We wish to thank Mr W. P. Le Clerc, Inspector of National Monuments, and Mr J. Bambury, Photographer to the National Monuments Branch of the Office of Public Works, Dublin, for their great helpfulness in the choice and provision of photographs of national monuments; Dr J. Raftery, Keeper of Irish Antiquities in the National Museum of Ireland, who was most helpful at all times; curators and librarians in various museums and libraries too numerous to mention, for the facilities they provided for the study of manuscripts and other antiquities in their care; Bord Fáilte Éireann for the gift of a large number of the photographs here used, and Cork Public Museum for Plate 17.

Almost all the museum objects here illustrated are housed in the National Museum of Ireland and we wish to thank the authorities of the National Museum not only for supplying the photographs attributed to them but also for permission to reproduce illustrations from other sources of objects in their care.

Finally we wish to express our thanks to Miss Joan Burns, B.A., for generous help in the preparation of the text for publication. To the general editor of the series, Dr Glyn Daniel, we owe much for stimulating editorship, good company and many kindnesses.

M. AND L. DE P.

ALL THE KINGS of Ireland, and the kings of the provinces, and even the petty kings of *tuatha* could trace their descent from Adam and Eve, naming an ancestor in each generation. They knew the names of all the races who had inhabited Ireland before themselves and that their own race had come from Spain; they even knew the full story of that migration of their forefathers and how it had come about. They knew in detail the history of the making of Ireland; who felled the first tree and who cleared the first plain and who ploughed the first furrow. Their knowledge was as full of colourful and minute detail as a children's fairy-tale and so long as their society, with its Celtic language and traditions, survived (as it did in part until the eighteenth century) this fairy-tale knowledge, precise and picturesque, was sufficient in itself, satisfying the curious by explaining at once the past and the present. There were learned classes, especially trained, privileged and protected, who preserved the memories of the race, transmitting their lore from generation to generation mainly by means of oral tradition. But there were occasions when these traditions were written down, either in full or in abbreviated mnemonic form, and thus many of them have been preserved to the present day. Particularly at times when the whole society was threatened, the custodians of traditional learning felt the need to commit their knowledge to writing. We have a great mass of legendary, topographical, historical, and genealogical material which was thus compiled and written down, first in the troubled eleventh and twelfth centuries, on the eve of the Norman invasion, and again in the seventeenth century, when, with the Gaelic society of Early Christian and Medieval Ireland already doomed, there was an extraordinary effort made by the survivors of the learned classes, by then, for the most part, uprooted, exiled, and work-ing in hardship and in poverty, to collect and preserve in print the ancient lore of Ireland.

> There is, indeed [as Plummer has written of them], hardly to be found in the history of literature a more pathetic tale than that of the way in which Colgan and his fellow-workers strove, amid poverty and persecution, and exile, to save the remains of their country's antiquities from destruction.[1]

But even in the seventeenth century it was a comparatively uncritical antiquarianism, and since then the hot breath of romance and the cold breath of criticism have dimmed the looking-glass world in which the past could once be seen with such clarity and colour. That glass was not history but poetry, and the reflection had its own truth. It showed the form which Celtic society had received from the mould of Ireland.

Ireland is, and was for long before it received its Celtic kings, an island in the ocean, lying far out from the shores of con-tinental Europe, beyond the long mountainous western coast of Britain. From a few vantage points on the east of Ireland one can see the British hills, but the headlands of the west offer prospects only of the ocean which, two thousand years ago, was the boundary of the known world and had no end. Save for a fifty-mile stretch of flat sandy shore on the east coast to the north of Dublin, the island of Ireland is rimmed with mountain-ranges, none of great height since they are ancient rocks which have been eroded by the blazing desert suns and scouring seas of Palaeozoic and Mesozoic times and ground down by the glaciers of the Ice Age, but formidable enough to make much of the coastline less accessible than the interior. The Atlantic tempers the winter's cold and the summer's heat, but all the year round cloud-banks drift eastward across the ocean to strike the western hills and there discharge their rain. Because of the configuration of the land only a small part of this

Fig. 1

Fig. 1. Map of Ireland showing physical features and royal sites. (High ground hatched, above 1,000 ft. cross-hatched.)

moisture can return directly to the sea; a great part of it drains into the rolling midland plain, which is thus waterlogged, so that central Ireland is a place of thousands of lakes, large and small, and many lonely tracts of bog. The plain is limestone and where the surface rises sufficiently above the water-table the lime is covered by a rich light soil, lush with grass, which provides some of the best grazing land in the world. But two thousand years ago these open ranges were fewer than now and the landscape was largely one of great forests, of oak, of ash, of elm, of hazel, and of yew. The flora and fauna were similar to those of Britain, but poorer; yet there was sufficient variety in the wild life abounding in the woods and bogs so that the country, with its mild climate, was then even more than now a land to please the hunter as well as the cattleman. These qualities seem to have been enhanced in the reputation the country enjoyed overseas, as the Venerable Bede's description, written in the eighth century, would suggest.

Ireland [he wrote], in breadth and for wholesomeness and serenity of climate far surpasses Britain; for the snow scarcely ever lies there above three days; no man makes hay in the Summer for Winter's provision or builds stables for his beasts of burden. No reptiles are found there and no snake can live there; for though often carried thither out of Britain, as soon as the ship comes near the shore and the scent of the air reaches them, they die. On the contrary, almost all things in the island are good against poison. In short, we have known that when some persons have been bitten by serpents, the scrapings of the leaves of books that were brought out of Ireland, being put into water and given to them to drink, have immediately expelled the spreading poison and assuaged the swelling. The island abounds in milk and honey; nor is there any want of vines, fish, or fowl; and it is remarkable for deer and goats.[2]

The very shape of the island makes for unity of culture, since the wide lowlands offer no formidable barrier to the spread of new fashions once they have become established in the country, while the highland periphery can provide only scattered and separate refuges for older traditions. At the same time centralization and uniformity are rendered difficult because the centre is commanded by so many natural fastnesses around its margin. So, from the beginning of recorded history there was unity of culture, of language, and of laws in Ireland, but not until comparatively modern times was a true centralization of political power and authority achieved. One of the remarkable features of early Irish literature is that there was a clear concept of Ireland as a nation, although, as in the other countries of Western Europe, the idea of the nation as a state lay far in the future. The historians were concerned to write, not the history of the most recent conquerors of the island, the Goidels, but the history of Ireland, and the widespread interest in antiquity arose only partly from pride of family and from the need, in a society where blood and kinship counted for so much in precedence, in rank, and in privilege, to keep careful genealogical accounts; it also derived in part from interest in the homeland itself and from pride in its culture. There was also interest in the past for its own sake, for the Irish are one of the most conservative of peoples, not unreceptive to new ideas, but with a considerable facility for absorbing the new into the old without the semblance of radical change, and an even more considerable tenacity of memory.

At the very moment when medieval Celtic society, with its traditions and its fanciful learning, died, it caught the imagination of Renaissance men, even before the Romantic interest in the Middle Ages had fully developed. Before the Elizabethan conquest had been brought to its bloody conclusion the lively and inquiring minds of the gentlemen adventurers who had made their way from England to Ireland turned to the past of the country in which they found themselves. Edmund Campion wrote a history of Ireland in 1571, and his friend Richard Stanyhurst attempted a 'Description of Ireland', both for Holinshed's *Chronicles*, and both almost worthless since their authors were quite unequipped for the task they undertook. Stanyhurst's nephew, James Ussher, Protestant Archbishop of Armagh from 1625 to 1656 and an alumnus of the newly founded Trinity College, Dublin, collected manuscripts and other antiquities and made some researches into Irish Church history. His work is much more scholarly and he was in communication with men who still retained some of the Gaelic tradition of learning. Sir James Ware, a pupil of Ussher, was another collector of manuscripts with a scholarly and sympathetic interest in Irish history, to working on which he devoted his life.

This interest in Irish antiquity which had been aroused in some members of the English-speaking Protestant Ascendancy continued through the eighteenth and into the nineteenth century. The publication in 1760 by the Scotsman James Macpherson of his translation of the 'Poems of Ossian' aroused a general interest in Celtic literature. Field antiquities in Ireland were studied by the Welshman Edward Lhwyd at the end of the seventeenth century, and later by Archdall, Ledwich, and others. At the same time there were still among the Irish-speaking Catholic population some few inheritors of the old Gaelic learning and tradition of the past; but the two groups remained separate and distinct in their interest in antiquity. On the one hand all was known precisely and in detail, although the knowledge was largely based on ancient fancy; on the other hand all was speculation, although the speculation was based, to some extent, on scholarship.

It was not until the early nineteenth century that the fruitful union of the two traditions was brought about. This occurred with the inauguration of the Ordnance Survey of Ireland. It was planned to supply, together with maps to a scale of six inches to the mile, memoirs describing the economic condition, resources, and antiquities of each county. George Petrie, a Dublin-born artist of Scottish descent, was placed in charge of the antiquities division in 1833 and he formed for this branch of the survey a committee consisting of John O'Donovan, Eugene O'Curry, W. F. Wakeman, and James Clarence Mangan. Their work on the survey was stopped by the Government shortly after it was begun, as being too expensive, but not before O'Donovan had compiled a series of notes in the field which are still of great value; moreover, most of these men continued their work on Irish antiquities. Petrie in an essay on the Round Towers of Ireland, read to the Royal Irish Academy, settled one of the questions which had been a cause of extraordinary speculation and acrimonious controversy; O'Donovan and O'Curry, both of them Irish speakers, performed prodigious labours in the editing and publishing of Irish manuscripts, and Wakeman published a number of papers on Early Christian Antiquities. At about this time also, in Ireland, as in England and on the Continent, archaeological societies were being founded, such as the Irish Archaeological Society, founded in 1840, while in Germany and France the growth of the new science of Comparative Philology had led to a critical study of the Celtic languages. O'Donovan and O'Curry had made shift to interpret Old Irish manuscripts in the light of their knowledge of modern Irish; now, after the publication of Zeuss's *Grammatica Celtica* in 1853, more accurate readings of Old Irish became possible.

From this time onward, as work on Irish antiquity became more critical, it became more specialized. The study of language, of ancient history, and of material remains of the past, each now became a special branch of learning. In the systematic study of material antiquities most valuable work was done by the brilliant Margaret Stokes, who edited posthumous

publications by Petrie on Christian Inscriptions in the Irish
Language and by Lord Dunraven on early Irish architecture,
as well as publishing papers of her own on Early Christian
sculpture, architecture, manuscript illumination, and metalwork in Ireland.

The Royal Irish Academy, since its foundation in 1782, had
sponsored researches into history and archaeology as well as
other branches of learning, and it had acquired a large collection
of antiquities, of prehistoric and early historic times. This
collection, later to be housed in the National Museum of
Ireland, was described systematically in a published catalogue
by Sir William Wilde, a busy Dublin surgeon who found
time to publish two books on field antiquities as well as this
major work of research.

O'Curry had been Professor of Irish History and Archaeology in the Catholic University of Ireland. On the foundation
of the National University in 1908, chairs of archaeology were
established in the constituent colleges at Dublin, Cork, and
Galway, and R. A. S. Macalister, who had done pioneer
research on the archaeology of Palestine, was appointed
Professor in Dublin.

In this century many scholars have worked on the antiquities
of Early Christian Ireland, concerning themselves chiefly with
the evolution of Irish art in this period. The pioneer work of
Petrie and Margaret Stokes was followed by that of T. J.
Westropp, H. S. Crawford, Dr Françoise Henry, whose two
brilliant books on the subject have provided a clear exposition
of the development of Irish art up to the ninth century, Dr H. G.
Leask, who has recently followed his many papers on architecture with the first volume of a book on *Irish Churches and
Monastic Buildings*, and other scholars working in Ireland, while
many chapters and papers on the subject have been contributed from other countries, notably by Shetelig, Åberg, Bøe,
Kendrick, and Clapham.

Although some unsystematic excavations of early historic sites were undertaken as early as the middle of the nineteenth century, the great wealth of material surviving in Ireland from the Early Christian period consisted until recent years either of stray finds, such as the Ardagh Chalice and the Tara brooch, or of shrines and other valuables which had remained in the hands of hereditary 'keepers' until they came into the possession of collectors or museums. As a result the stress has been mainly on the study of art, and researches into the life of Early Christian Ireland have depended mainly on written sources, although an attempt was made by Joyce in his *A Social History of Ancient Ireland*—an unfortunately uncritical work published in 1903— to make use of the material antiquities to illustrate the course of everyday life.

Plates 19, 22

The Harvard Archaeological Mission, which came to Ireland in 1933 and has done so much also to further the study of Irish prehistory, made systematic excavations of Early Christian sites, principally the lake-dwellings at Lagore and Ballinderry, and in the quarter-century since then many other habitation sites of the period have been scientifically excavated, yielding much valuable information. In many ways the most important of these was the ring-fort at Garranes, Co. Cork, excavated by the late Professor Ó Ríordáin shortly before the war.

Researches into the Irish past from the time of the coming of Christianity in the fifth century until the 'far Western Christian civilization'—as Toynbee has called it—was fatally assaulted by the Anglo-Normans in the late twelfth century, have there-fore now reached the point where a summary of the culture of the period may be attempted, although there is still much that must remain obscure. To apply the term 'Early Christian' to a period as late as the twelfth century may seem misleading, but until the effects of the Gregorian reform of the Church became fully felt in Ireland about the middle of that century, it is true to say that there was little in the ecclesiastical affairs of Ireland which would have seemed strange to the Desert Fathers of the primitive Church while secular affairs observed a more primitive order still and would have seemed familiar to Julius Caesar who had seen the shipping of the Veneti and had faced the impetuous onslaught of the Britons. Indeed, although the Irish Church took on a fully medieval character in the twelfth century, Irish secular society kept something of the character of the Celtic Iron Age as long as it retained any independence. When the last descendants of the Celtic kings had sailed from the shores of eighteenth-century Ireland, the last of the poets, of the race of genealogists and historians who had lived well in their royal houses, Aodhagán Ó Rathaille, sick, destitute, alone, too proud to recite the praises of any but 'the sons of the kings', wrapped the cloak of his poverty around him and sang his last song—

> . . . I will cease now, death is nigh unto me without delay;
> Since the warriors of the Laune, of Lein, and of the Lee
> have been laid low,
> I will follow the beloved among the heroes to the grave,
> Those princes under whom were my ancestors before the
> death of Christ.[3]

CHAPTER I

Ireland and Rome

I<small>N THE SUMMER</small> of A.D. 82 Cnaeus Julius Agricola, governor of Britain, having conquered all the tribes south of the Forth and the Clyde, now assembled his forces 'in that part of Britain which looks towards Ireland'. He had nothing to fear from the west but rather, as his son-in-law tells us, was eager for future conquests. 'I have often heard Agricola say', writes Tacitus, 'that Ireland could be invaded and conquered with one legion and a moderate number of auxiliaries. The result would be of advantage even with reference to the coercion of Britain, if Roman arms were to be seen everywhere and independence swept from the map.'[1] But the independence whose destruction was so confidently envisaged by the victorious Roman general was not to disappear for another thousand years. Agricola changed his plans and Ireland alone of the western nations did not come under Roman sway. The story of Early Christian Ireland is, in the main, the story of the gradual absorption of Mediterranean culture by an unsubdued Celtic community, who yielded, not to Roman arms, but to Roman letters and religion.

EARLY CONTACTS WITH ROME

The arrival of peaceful missionaries in the fifth century marks the real beginning of this process but already in the time of Tacitus the Roman world had some contacts with Ireland. 'The interior parts', he says, 'are little known, but through commercial intercourse and the merchants there is better knowledge of the harbours and approaches.' In Ireland itself the archaeological evidence supplements this written testimony. Roman objects, few in number as one might expect of casual imports, are known from every century of the Roman occupation of Britain, and the objects indicate a heightened activity at two periods in particular: the first century and the fourth century.

With a group of crouched burials on Lambay Island, off the east coast near Dublin, were found five bronze brooches and an iron mirror as well as Iron Age objects. Four of the brooches are Roman; the fifth is of particular interest since it is a barbarian copy of a Roman fibula. The craftsman has carefully reproduced the form but has misunderstood the mechanism, casting the pin, which should be movable, to the catchplate. Already the Celtic metalworkers (in this case possibly working in Wales) were imitating Roman objects. The entire group of relics, including a fine repoussé disc, belongs to the first century A.D. and it has been suggested that the burials were those of refugees fleeing from the Roman invasion of Wales. More solid evidence for trade is provided by Samian and Arretine potsherds of this date at the crannogs of Ballinderry and Lagore, while recent excavations at the royal site of Tara have yielded Roman material of the first four centuries—pottery, glass, and the lead filling for a seal-box. An *olla*, dredged up a hundred and fifty miles off the west coast of Ireland, indicates that trade (in wine or oil) was not confined to the Irish Sea. In exchange for these commodities the export of Irish wolfhounds for use in public amusements is known from references by several Roman writers, one of whom, Symmachus, thought that 'they must have been brought in iron cages',[2] such was their ferocity. A small bronze model of one of these magnificent animals was found in the excavations at Lydney Park in Gloucestershire, indicating the extent to which they took the fancy of their purchasers. Export of hides and cattle are also mentioned in the literature.

Plate 3

The Roman finds from the fourth and fifth centuries, however, cannot all be explained as the result of peaceful commerce. The empire, now in its decline, was a tempting prey for
barbarian enemies, among whom the Picts and the Scots are
mentioned by several Roman writers. 'The Picts and Saxons
and Scots (Irish) and Atecotti harassed the Britons with con-
tinual afflictions', writes Ammianus of A.D. 365, while the
Irish traditions make it clear that plunder and slaves were
sought across the Irish Sea. Niall of the Nine Hostages, the
first high king of Ireland whose historical existence is
generally accepted, is described in a poem as having led seven
expeditions across the sea, and his mother Cairenn is said to
have been a British captive. Again the archaeological evidence
dramatically bears out the literary. Looted Roman silver
deposited in the early fifth century—coins, ingots, and plate,
savagely hacked by the barbarian raiders—has been found at
Coleraine in the north and Balline in the south. At Balline the   Plate 4
makers' stamps clearly show that some of the material came
from Britain.

It was from Britain also that an Irish raiding party, some time
in the early fifth century, carried off into slavery in Ulster the
young son of a provincial Roman official. This was the young
Patrick who was to be renowned as the apostle of Ireland.

ST PATRICK

Traditions and legends of St Patrick collected by pious
hagiographers of the seventh century and later medieval times
have been preserved, but the fifth-century records are so meagre
and so confusing that there has been much controversy as to
the exact date of his arrival in Ireland, the date of his death,
and the extent of his share in the conversion of the country.

Prosper of Aquitaine records in his *Chronicle* that Pope Celestine in the year 431 sent Palladius to minister to 'those of the Irish who believed in Christ'. The Irish annals record the arrival of Patrick in Ireland in A.D. 432, but they give two dates for his death, 461 and 493. The traditional view of the saint's career (as expounded by Bury) was that Palladius for some reason failed in his mission and was followed immediately by Patrick, who lived and worked in Ireland until 461. The second entry of his death is attributed to an annalistic error. In 1941 the late Professor T. F. O'Rahilly put forward the opinion that there were two Patricks, each working for about thirty years as a missionary in Ireland, the elder, who died in 461 being known as Palladius, the younger being Patrick the Briton, who came at about the time of the death of Palladius and who died in 493. A more recent view has been advanced by Professor J. Carney, who accepts much of O'Rahilly's critical reassessment of the sources but who believes that the early Irish traditions were correct in being aware of only one Patrick engaged in the conversion of Ireland—the British Patrick, who came to Ireland about the year 456 and died in 493. The controversy continues and no end to it is in sight, since the philologists agree only in correcting the slovenly transcription of the annalistic scribes and agree not at all in their corrections. In a recent critical discussion of the controversy, Mario Esposito has proposed another solution—that Patrick the Briton preceded Palladius and died in about 430 at the end of a fairly successful mission.

Fortunately Patrick the Briton has left a document which not only supplies an outline of his early career but conveys something of his character as a man. This is his *Confessio*,[3] written in his old age as a spiritual *apologia*. It is a simple but moving work which tells how he was carried off while still a boy from the civilized life of a Roman villa to the remote and barbarous hills of Ireland where, for six years, he was to herd flocks for his Irish master. At the end of that period an angelic voice spoke to him on the mountainside announcing that the time had come for him to escape from his servitude: 'Lo, thy ship is ready.' The ship, he tells us, lay two hundred miles from his place of captivity. It was a merchant vessel bound for Gaul with a cargo of dogs and it made the journey in three days; but this was the calamitous fifth century, the barbarians had crossed the Rhine and Patrick and his seafaring companions found Gaul a smoking desert in which they nearly perished for want of food. It was after many vicissitudes that he succeeded in rejoining his family in Britain, intending to remain there. But he tells us that he saw visions and again heard a voice, 'the Voice of the Irish' crying 'as with one mouth, "We beseech thee, holy youth, to come hither and walk among us."' He took this to be a command of God that he should go to convert the heathen in Ireland. He was ordained priest and prepared himself for his mission; though apparently opposed and prevented for some time by his ecclesiastical superiors, he finally, with what companions and with what support he does not record, set sail for Ireland.

Apart from Prosper's reference in A.D. 431 to 'those Irish who believed in Christ', there is evidence to suggest that there were some Christians, probably few in number, in Ireland before the start of Patrick's mission. Early genealogies and lives of the Irish saints preserve traditions of pre-Patrician Christianity among the peoples of the south coast; the Corcu Loegde in Cork and the Dési in Waterford. But in the *Confessio* Ireland is depicted as an almost wholly pagan country although Patrick in speaking of his journeys there, some of which were 'even to outlying regions beyond which no man dwelt, and where never had anyone come to baptize or ordain clergy, or confirm the people', might seem to imply that there were other regions where people had come to baptize, ordain, and confirm.

It is with the midlands, the north, and the west that the name of Patrick is especially associated in tradition, but the same traditions are clear in attributing the main credit for the conversion of Ireland to him. His conquest of Ireland for the Christian faith, according to the early writers, was almost bloodless (the many legends of his life tell of only one martyr) and was accomplished with the equivalent of even less than 'one legion and a moderate number of auxiliaries'. This was a remarkable achievement and Patrick, who seems to have been, like St Teresa of Avila many centuries later, a combination of mystic and able administrator, was the first to demonstrate in practice that Christianity was an institution which would break the bounds and survive the end of the Roman Empire.

FIFTH-CENTURY IRELAND

It is well to remember that in Ireland, for the first time in the west, Christianity was established in a wholly barbarian community, with the result that the Church organization, related as it was to the urban organization of the Empire, did not long retain its character. The country at the time of its conversion was still in an heroic age with a pre-literate Iron Age culture at a more primitive stage of development than that which Julius Caesar had found in Gaul five centuries before. Our knowledge of Ireland as it was in St Patrick's time and for some centuries before must depend on the archaeological material, which is disappointingly meagre for this period, and on the immense body of literature, surviving in manuscripts chiefly of the twelfth century and later, but incorporating some material derived directly from the oral traditions of the pre-Patrician age. The early sagas supply the most vivid picture of life in Ireland before St Patrick. In them we find depicted a pagan people, speaking a Celtic language and living in a state of society recently described by a Celtic scholar as 'tribal, rural, hierarchical and familiar'. Kingship, which was disappearing in Gaul by the first century B.C., survived in Ireland, and the king, besides being a ruler, was in some sense a sacred person, descended from the ancestral god of his tribe and entering on his rule by taking part in inauguration rites whereby he became the embodiment of his people, bound by many magical *gessa*, or tabus, and responsible not merely for his own conduct as a ruler but for the fertility of the land and for protecting his tribe against blight and plague of every sort. There were many of these kings in the country, each ruling his own *tuath*, or tribe, on its ancestral lands, and paying tribute to the over king who ruled a province. By St Patrick's time the two principal over kings were established at Tara and Cashel, but there are indications that this was a fairly recent development.

According to the oldest Irish traditions the peoples who inhabited the country in historical times had come in a series of invasions and there had been much fighting for the richer lands of the plains of the east midlands and the plains of north Munster. By the fifth century A.D. something of a balance of power had been achieved between the Ui Néill (descendants of King Niall Noígiallach), the dynasty of overlords who had established themselves at Tara in the midlands and who claimed the sovereignty of Ireland, although their sway was effective only in the northern half of the country, and the Eoghanachta (descendants of Eógan) who were established at Cashel in the plain of Tipperary and claimed the overlordship of the southern half of the country. Throughout the fifth century and into the sixth the Ui Néill of Tara were still engaged in conflict with the Lagin (the people of Leinster) the older possessors of the midland plain, whom they finally dislodged from *Mide* (i.e. Westmeath) in A.D. 513. Previously there seem to have been five separate kingdoms (the Irish word

Fig. 1

for province means literally a 'fifth') but in the historical period there were seven, three of them being fragments of the old northern kingdom of the *Ulaid*. Warfare on the frontier of the *Ulaid* is the theme of the main body of the saga-literature and the stories are full of accounts of customs and of things which had disappeared when Christianity was established: fighting from chariots; the power and prestige of druids and seers; the taking of human heads in combat; and the mythological Otherworld of the Celt.

The early fifth century therefore saw not only the introduction of Christianity to the whole of Ireland but the shaping of the political structure that was to endure for five centuries. Tara and Cashel remained paramount in their respective spheres of influence; the Eoghanacht dynasty which came into control in the south some time about the year 400 maintained the sovereignty of Munster until the middle of the tenth century, and the high-kingship remained in the hands of the Ui Néill until it was usurped by Brian Boru in the year 1002. At no time was the sovereignty of the high king well defined, but he claimed suzerainty over the seven petty kingdoms whose rulers in turn exacted tribute from minor chiefs (of *tuatha*) to the total number of about a hundred.

The economy of this society was pastoral and agricultural. There were no cities or towns. Archaeological evidence for the immediately pre-Christian period is extremely meagre, but it seems likely that the hill-forts of the Iron Age were passing out of use in St Patrick's time. Groups of earthworks mark the royal sites of Tara, Emain Macha, and Cruachain, but so far only one of these earthworks has been excavated. The Rath of the Synods at Tara, a triple-ramparted ring-fort, was a stockaded enclosure with wooden buildings and it seems likely that the typical unit of society was already, as in Christian times, the isolated homestead—ring-fort or crannog—and St Patrick's early foundations were based on this model.

Fig. 1
Plate 3

Although not all the Irish kings accepted Christianity from Patrick—Loiguire the high king, among others, remaining pagan—there was little opposition to his ministry and he was permitted to move through the country, baptizing, confirming, ordaining clergy, and founding churches. He speaks of 'count, less numbers' of converts and many of the petty kings are recorded as making grants of land for the building of churches. No fifth-century church has survived but accounts in the literature give a picture of such an establishment. A circular enclosure similar to the ring-fort surrounded a group of three buildings—a large dwelling-house for the clerics, a church or oratory where Mass was said and a kitchen which was perhaps also used as a refectory. These centres of ecclesiastical rule were governed by bishops and were known as 'cities' by analogy with the Roman *civitates* which were the bishops' seats every, where else in Christendom. It must be remembered that the Church organization as established by Patrick was not monastic: in numerous cases he is described as placing bishops and priests in charge of churches but only one instance is recorded of a church being handed over to an abbot. Never, theless, the idea of monasticism was already finding considerable favour in Patrick's time amongst both men and women. 'The sons of the Irish and the daughters of chieftains who were monks and virgins of Christ I am unable to enumerate', he writes, and we can infer from the documents that these pious converts were placed in small groups to assist the clerics. In any case the ecclesiastical settlements were organized from the beginning rather in the nature of monastic communities and the transition cannot have been difficult from the larger foundations such as Armagh or Sletty to the more formal monasteries of later times. In the primatial see of Armagh such a change had already taken place before the end of the fifth century.

Plate 15

The fifth-century missionaries brought the use of letters to Ireland, and the historical period is commonly dated from their coming, but our knowledge of the following century remains very defective. The mission, although it brought something of Roman culture to Ireland, could not make of the country a cultural province of the Empire because the Imperial civilization in the west was already being destroyed. On New Year's Eve in A.D. 406 the Vandals, Alans, and Sueves had crossed the frozen Rhine to ransack Gaul from the frontier to the Pyrenees; Rome itself had been plundered by Goths and slaves in A.D. 410; the legions had withdrawn from Britain, abandoning that country to the incursions of Irish, Picts, and Saxons. Everywhere in the western provinces the chroniclers of the fifth century retail a dreary list of battles, sieges, the sacking and burning of cities, whilst the wanderings of barbarian armies to and fro across Europe can be traced, but we lack a detailed knowledge of the cultural and social history of this time of troubles. Yet the destruction of a rich and mighty civilization was not accomplished overnight; life went on in spite of Vandals and Huns, as it has gone on in twentieth-century Europe despite the devastation of civilized cities from the air.

In Ireland the terse annalistic entries of the fifth and sixth centuries tell us a little of the doings of kings and chiefs in their perpetual sport of cattle-reiving and frontier-skirmishing, but there is scant information of the great process by which the country was made Christian and literate, acquired scholarship of a relatively high order, and, undisturbed by the mighty downfall of Rome, developed the rich art and literature of its Golden Age. The seemingly sudden appearance, at the close of the seventh century, of a developed and complex Irish art with little to show by way of immediate antecedents but at the same time displaying a remarkable revival of the spirit of the art of the Iron Age makes the understanding of this difficult period all the more necessary. The obscurity of English history in the century following the withdrawal of the legions and of the early history of Christianity in Ireland adds to the difficulties, and there has been much controversy, too often accompanied by the display of an inappropriate nationalistic bias, as to whether early 'Celtic' art-styles survived in unconquered Ireland or were kept alive by British craftsmen in the less thoroughly Romanized parts of their island. The evidence now available seems to support neither of the extreme views main-tained in this controversy. Many of the problems have not yet been solved, but we must try here to summarize the evidence from all sources and, while space will not permit full dis-cussion of the many controversial questions, to present an outline of the developments which led to the cultural achieve-ments of the eighth century.

Both in Great Britain and in Ireland a splendid curvilinear abstract art, of late La Tène antecedents, had appeared on metal objects of the Iron Age. The Irish style is closely related to that of Britain but has its own individual character. It appears in its earliest form on sword-scabbards from the crannog of Lisnacrogher, Co. Antrim, which was destroyed in the nineteenth century, and on similar scabbards from Coleraine, Co. Derry and from the river Bann at Toome. These are decorated with incised curvilinear ornament of S-shaped or scroll forms, highly stylized palmettes, small tightly coiled 'hairspring' spirals, and basketry hatching. Similar curvilinear patterns appear on a slightly later series of objects in repoussé metal work; among the finest of these are the gold collar from Broighter, Co. Derry, the bronze trumpet from Lough-na-Shade, Co. Armagh and an unlocalized bronze disc. This was an aristocratic art, in Britain associated with the second phase of the Early Iron Age there and represented in one of its sub-styles on the

Plate 1

equipment of the warlords who were buried with their fighting-chariots in Yorkshire. In Ireland, while the archaeological material is too meagre for the identification of any large-scale invasion, we may at least infer the existence of elements of a culture of La Tène type, and there is some evidence from the archaeological material and a great deal more from the early saga literature for the use of the two-horse war chariot.

An art which had already reached perfection within its own conventions could only decline, and in Britain this art was already well past its prime when the invasion fleet of Claudius set sail. In Ireland the quality remained high in the horse-bits and other objects marking the later stages of the style but the curvilinear patterns were less complex, until finally, about the early third century A.D., they faded out of use altogether. In Scotland the last Iron Age style, exemplified in a series of massive bracelets, came to an end at about the same time.

Of equal importance with the predilection for curvilinear forms in the later revival of Celtic taste in art was the craft of enamelling which had been diffused in Europe by the La Tène cultures. Little balls or plaques of coral had been used by the early La Tène metalworkers in Europe to enrich the equipment and personal ornaments of the warrior chieftains. Perhaps because of the increasing scarcity of coral these began to be replaced in the third century B.C. by small studs of red glass (a ring-headed pin, of similar form to coral-mounted pins at Kilham, Yorkshire, and Hammersmith but with just such a glass stud replacing the coral, was found at Lisnacrogher) and soon true enamelling in champlevé appeared on the metalwork. Small fields of red champlevé enamel occur on some of the Lisnacrogher pieces and on most of the Iron Age horse furniture found in Ireland. In the Belgic areas of Britain the enamelling of much larger areas of champlevé was attempted and shortly before the Claudian invasion other colours besides red were introduced, although in the form of small pieces of coloured glass set in the red enamel, as on the harness-mount from Westhall in Suffolk. At about the time of the Conquest, or shortly after, true yellow enamel appeared in England, inspired probably by provincial fibulae from the Continent, and in Scotland some of the massive bracelets made in the second century have chequer patterns in red and yellow enamel, while other objects, such as a bridle-bit from Burnswark, have small triangular panels of champlevé enamel like those common on provincial Roman jewellery. The Iron Age tradition in enamelling and in art-forms can be traced down almost to the fourth century A.D., when it is finally eclipsed in Britain by the mass-production and rather lifeless Classical art-forms of Roman culture, while in Ireland apparently the art declined from intrinsic causes.

All along the Roman frontier, and in some of the provinces, especially Gaul, the minor arts of metal-working and enamel-ling seem to have remained in the hands of barbarian craftsmen, who conservatively retained in their work reminiscences of Iron Age forms. A hybrid style in small openwork and enamelled metal objects resulted, compounded of some classical elements and the curvilinear and asymmetrical tendencies of La Tène art, which lasted until the catastrophic barbarian incursions of the middle of the third century A.D. This style is not so evident in Britain but there are some examples of it. Working in a fairly thoroughly Romanized society the Celtic bronzesmiths and enamellers still retained their delight in the restless and mobile forms of the earlier art, and, as Leeds has pointed out, this may be observed even in the treatment of the ornamental motifs of the potters in the Caistor and New Forest wares. Roman culture penetrated the Highland Zone of Britain less thoroughly than the Lowlands, and most of Scot-land remained outside the province.

In the third century Britain was prosperous, peaceful, and Roman; towards the end of the century the Irish from the west, the Picts from the north, and the Saxons from the east began raiding the province and, in spite of Roman defence measures, the attacks increased in vigour until, in the fourth century, the barbarians formed an alliance and, invading Britain simul- taneously from all sides, swept over the whole country, looting and devastating. Late in the century Hadrian's Wall was evacuated and early in the following century the Romans finally abandoned Britain. Apart from the testimony of Roman writers as to these alliances and warlike movements of the barbarian peoples, there is abundant evidence to show that at this time—the fourth and early fifth centuries—there was great activity in the Highland Zone and especially an expansive energy in Ireland. From Ulster at about this time warriors of the Dál Riata sept began their conquests in the land of the Picts, which were to bring the culture and language of Ireland into Scotland; from southern Ireland large numbers of colonists —largely, it would seem, of the Dési of Munster—crossed the Channel to Wales, hot on the heels of the departing Roman garrison. Ship-loads of Angles and Saxons were already dis- embarking on the east coast as the Romans left, and the Britons, advised by the Emperor, to whom they appealed, to look to their own defence, found themselves desperately caught between two invasions. But they held the west country, pre- vented a large-scale colonization of North Wales by the Irish, and retained their identity for some time in a number of small kingdoms before these were finally reduced, as far as the present Welsh border, by the Anglo-Saxons.

It was in this obscure period that 'Celtic' art was revived and we must not look to any one part of the Highland Zone, where there was constant movement to and fro across the Irish Sea, for the origins of the revived style, which springs from the same fourth-century renewal of barbarian vigour that was to be the downfall of Roman Britain.

THE REVIVAL OF METALWORKING

This revival in Ireland was associated with the appearance of types of metal objects derived from Britain. Of these, the most important types were the series of 'hand-pins' and the penannular brooches, which form the chief links with the later metalwork of the Christian period, but the tentative beginnings of the new style appeared on other objects made in this Dark Age. A bronze spiral bracelet found in the Boyne has a simple whorl, probably in red champlevé enamel similar to the patterns of the earliest ornamented hand-pins and brooches; a bronze hooked toilet-implement of Roman type found in Ireland has a circular panel of red enamel with a similar design; a few finger-rings of Roman inspiration—from Rathbally, Co. Wicklow and from Co. Cavan—were also ornamented in this fashion, while an unlocalized finger-ring in the National Museum of Ireland has a rectangular bezel with red enamel in which are set small pieces of blue glass, and another ring from Ballinard, Co. Limerick, is a very early example in Ireland of the use of millefiori glass set in enamel.

Figs. 2, 3

Until the late seventh century, enamelling in Ireland seems to have been in red only, but at a much earlier date it became possible to add other colours to metalwork by means of little plaques of millefiori glass set in enamel. This was made rather after the fashion of the long sticks of two- or three-coloured toffee that are sold in seaside towns: glass heated to a semi-solid state was drawn out in long rods; different colours were then fused together in a bundle and again drawn out into a single rod; finally, when this had cooled, small slices were cut from it, each revealing a multi-coloured cross-section. Skilful workers could produce quite elaborate and minute patterns in this medium. The technique was of oriental origin but had been practised by glass-workers in the western Empire in the second and third centuries A.D. The number of places of

Plates 20, 21

manufacture is unknown; there was one factory in Belgium near Namur, and there may have been others in the Western Empire; but it seems that production had virtually ceased in all of them by the end of the third century. It is most likely that some of the glass-workers made their way to Britain and Ireland; a bronze stud with millefiori ornament was found in a fourth-century context at Chesterholm, Northumberland, and in the sixth century A.D. millefiori was being manufactured at Garranes, Co. Cork.

The dress-ornaments known as hand-pins (from the slight resemblance which they bear, in the developed form with five studs, to a clenched fist) have a long ancestry, extending back into the Early Iron Age or perhaps (if Mahr's suggestion that their form was influenced by the sunflower pin is correct) into an even more remote period of antiquity. The form whence they have been derived is the so-called 'swan's-neck pin', a simple dress-fastening consisting of a long shaft pointed at the lower end and bent into an S-shape at the top. This being utilitarian rather than ornamental, the craftsmen improved on it by bending the upper member of the S into a circle to produce a ring-headed pin with a cranked shaft, and soon the ring was ornamented with small pellets. Further refinement of this form led to the development of several different types of pin; in one of these the lower half of the ring was formed as a flat lunate panel and the upper half consisted of three small pellets. This form was achieved in northern Britain in the period from the third to the sixth century A.D. and examples of this prototype of the hand-pin have been found in the hill-top site of Traprain Law and also at Norrie's Law, both in Scotland, while pins of the same form have been found in Ireland. The lower panel of the bronze ring, at this stage of development, was ornamented with very simple curvilinear patterns—triskeles or whorls—showing as a reserve of bronze against a background of red champlevé enamel. The final

Fig. 2. A hand-pin from Armagh. 8¾ in. long.

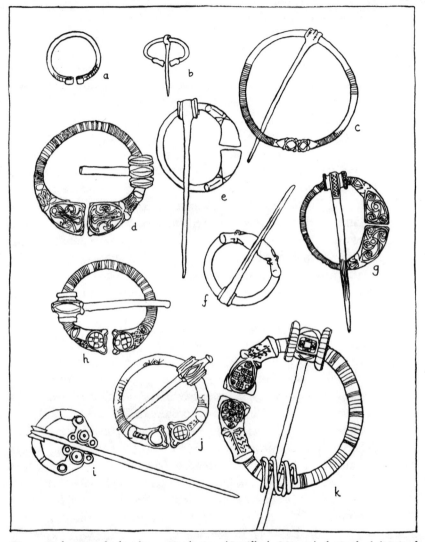

Fig. 3. Early penannular brooches. a. Verulamium (St Alban's Museum); b. Scotland (National Museum of Antiquities, Edinburgh); c. Ford of Toome, Lough Neagh (British Museum); d. Co. Antrim (British Museum); e. Belleisle, Co. Fermanagh (N M I); f-j. No locality, Ireland (N M I); k. Ballinderry Crannog No. 2 (N M I). k—3 in. in diameter. Others to scale.

Fig. 2

Fig. 3

development of the type took place in Ireland. The number of studs was increased to five, now arranged in a horizontal row of projecting tubes of bronze, each with an enamel filling; the open space within the ring was gradually diminished to a pin-point and then dispensed with altogether; the lunate plate was given greater prominence and enlarged to a semicircle, although its decoration remained fairly simple, consisting usually of curvilinear patterns symmetrically arranged around the vertical axis. Hand-pins of this form continued to be made until as late as the eighth century.

Small penannular brooches of a very simple form were already in use in southern Britain when the Romans came, and continued to be manufactured there during the early centuries of the occupation. These consisted of two members: a wire hoop with rolled-back terminals, and a short pin, also of wire, attached by a loop at the top of the hoop. The craftsmen of the west, probably about the end of the third century, began to adapt this simple brooch to their own taste; they folded back the terminals of the hoop and clinched the fold with pincers; the shape thus given to the folded ends suggested to them the head of an animal and soon they began to manufacture the brooches with stylized animal protoms, following an old tradition of Iron Age metalworking which had been kept alive in Roman Britain in the ornament of fire-dogs, cauldron-handles, and similar features of domestic ironwork. Where precisely this innovation in the form of the penannular brooch took place is uncertain, because, like the other new forms of the period, it was rapidly diffused over a wide area, and penannular brooches in the initial zoomorphic stage have been found in Ireland, Scotland, and Wales. Once the innovation was made, however, its ornamental possibilities were exploited. Heavier brooches, of bronze or silver, were made by casting; the terminals were enlarged to stress their zoomorphic form and the hoop was decorated with incisions or grooves. When this

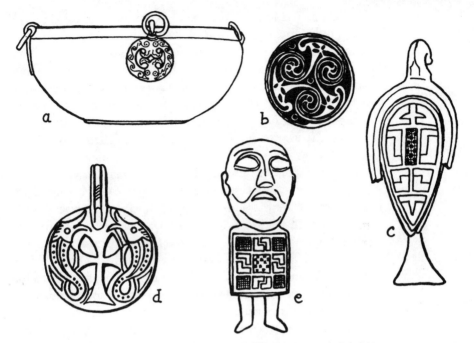

Fig. 4. Hanging-bowl and escutcheons. a. Baginton (Coventry Museum); b. Oving (Aylesbury Museum); c. Hopperstad (Bergens Museum); d. Faversham (British Museum); e. Myklebostad (Bergens Museum). Different scales.

stage was reached the enamellers found that the brooches offered scope to their craft and brooches were cast with recesses for champlevé enamel on the zoomorphic terminals. The provision of this field for the art of the enameller then came to be the predominant consideration in the design of some of the brooches; the terminals were greatly enlarged, being hammered out flat after casting, and the animal features were sometimes lost completely or reduced to a few vestigial lines. Like the hand-pins, but in much greater variety of style and ornament, the penannular brooches with zoomorphic terminals continued to be manufactured until the eighth century.

43

Fig. 4a

All the techniques and patterns of the hand-pins and penannular brooches appear in greater perfection on another series of objects which spans the period from Roman times until the developed art of the eighth century. These are large hemispherical bowls of beaten bronze with three or four hooks around the rim to enable them to be suspended from chains. They are commonly known as 'hanging-bowls', but their function is uncertain. The most usual explanation offered is that they were *gabatae* or hanging oil-lamps of a type that is known to have been used in Early Christian churches on the Continent, but, as has been recently suggested by Leistol, there are several reasons for preferring to interpret them as hand-basins, which could have had either a secular use or a use in the liturgy of the Mass. Commonly there is an elaborately ornamented disc on the bottom of the bowl, richly decorated on the interior, and it seems unlikely that this was intended for a position where it would be concealed under viscous oil. One of the bowls from Sutton Hoo has a bronze fish, cast in the round, and mounted in the interior of the vessel; the natural element of this creature should be water and it seems even more unlikely that he was intended to swim in dark oil. A simple hanging-bowl recently found in Norway bore an inscription in runes reading: I MUNTLAUKU—'in (the) hand-basin . . .'. Finally, indirect evidence is supplied by a panel at the end of one of the arms of Muiredach's Cross at Monasterboice, where a scene, usually interpreted as Pilate washing his hands, is carved; in this the water-holding vessel is clearly a hanging-bowl.

Whatever their function, these bowls were manufactured and used in Roman Britain and their subsequent history illustrates the darkness and confusion of the ensuing Age of Migrations. The earliest bowls, found on Roman sites in England and on the Continent, were spun on a pole-lathe; they are of simple but graceful form, of rather shallow proportions,

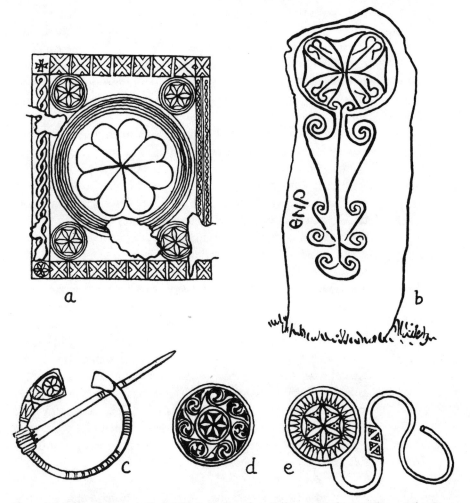

Fig. 5. Marigolds and rosettes in Early Irish art. a. Page from Bobbio ms. (Ambrosian Library, Milan, D. 23. sup.); b. Incised slab at Reask, Co. Kerry; c. Penannular brooch from Ireland (Ashmolean Museum); d. Escutcheon from hanging-bowl from Baginton (Coventry Museum); e. Latchet from Newry, Co. Down (British Museum). Different scales.

Fig. 4

each with three hooks cast in the form of birds or animals. In late Roman times deeper, hemispherical bowls, with slightly in-turned rims and with openwork escutcheons—usually a combination of peltas—were made. Escutcheons from bowls of this type have been found in Scotland, and one in the river Bann in Ireland; these may well have been carried away as loot from southern England.

After the departure of the Romans from England hanging-bowls continued to be manufactured. The earliest of the post-Roman bowls are of rather thick beaten bronze, with in-turned rims and with escutcheons whose ornament consists of wiry curvilinear patterns in red enamel. These have been found not on Roman sites but in pagan Saxon graves: yet it is clear that they are not of Saxon workmanship. They were made in the Celtic west—whether in Ireland or in Britain has long been the subject of controversy. Rather later bowls, of the late sixth and seventh centuries, are of very thin beaten bronze, with folded rims and with escutcheons bearing elaborate curvilinear patterns of red, yellow and blue champlevé enamel. These also have been found in Saxon graves. The last group of bowls, with patterns in red and yellow enamel and in millefiori on the escutcheons and with rims rolled over a wire core, have been found in early ninth-century Viking graves in Norway, and their source is almost certainly Ireland. Therefore it seems that the hanging-bowls were being made in Ireland in the eighth century, but when they first began to be made there it is impossible to say.

The evidence supplied by the three classes of objects described above—hand-pins, penannular brooches, and hanging-bowls—is supplemented by that of other secular objects of the same period. There is, for example, a series of small penannular-headed pins with ornithomorphic terminals which seem to trace their descent from a British type of the late Roman period. There is also a series of objects, usually known as

'latchets', which were probably dress-fasteners; they have Plate 5
curvilinear patterns, sometimes in enamel. All the evidence con-
verges to suggest that there is really little in Irish art, beyond the
mere tradition of working in bronze and enamel, deriving
directly from the Iron Age, but that metalworking in the west
received a powerful stimulus from provincial Roman work in
Britain, and that the result of this stimulus was a revived art in
the fifth and sixth centuries, in the Highland Zone. This art
was mainly secular. It coincides with the eclipse of Roman
power and culture in Britain and it rapidly acquired a specifically 'Celtic' expression, giving new life to the dying elements of
La Tène art which still lingered on in the west. Its inspiration
and beginnings were largely in Britain but it was developed in
Ireland, which lay beyond the reach of the Saxon invaders. Its
forms were elegant and lively but its repertoire was not extensive
until it came into the service of the most vigorous institution of
the age—the Church—and until it received a further stimulus in
the seventh century from the art and crafts of the Anglo-Saxons.

THE PATRICIAN CHURCH

Of the progress of Christianity in the immediately post-
Patrician period little can be said. No contemporary records
survive, but the traditional view of the period up to A.D. 544
is summarized (and stylized) by the eighth-century *Catalogue
of the Saints of Ireland.*

The first order of Catholic saints [according to this
document], was in the time of Patrick; and then they were all
bishops, distinguished and holy, and full of the Holy Ghost,
350 in number, founders of churches. They had one head,
Christ, and one chief, Patrick. They had one Mass, one

liturgy, one tonsure from ear to ear. They celebrated one Easter, on the fourteenth moon after the vernal equinox, and what was excommunicated by one church all excommunicated. They did not reject the service and society of women because founded on the rock, Christ, they feared not the blast of temptation. This order of saints lasted for four reigns, those namely of Loiguire, of Ailill Molt, of Lugaid son of Loiguire, and of Tuathal. All these bishops are sprung from the Romans and Franks and Britons and Scots.[4]

No material remains are known to have survived of this premonastic Irish Church. The celebration of the *feis* of Tara, which seems to have been a pagan inauguration ceremony involving the idea of the marriage of the king with Tara, or with the sovereignty, is not recorded in the reigns of Lugaid, Muirchertach, or Tuathal, but the High King Diarmait mac Cerbaill celebrated the *feis* in A.D. 560. There are many legends of conflict between Diarmait and ecclesiastics, and it seems probable that his reign marked the final resistance of paganism in Ireland. Christianity triumphed. Tara, according to legend, was cursed by St Ruadán of Lorrha, who had quarrelled with Diarmait, and was abandoned thereafter by the kings. Diarmait himself was defeated in A.D. 561 in the battle of *Cúl Dreimne*, and his defeat was brought about, according to the *Annals of Ulster*, 'through the prayers of St Columcille'. Whatever may lie behind the legends, the century from about 460 to about 560 seems to have seen the great change wrought in Ireland from a pagan Iron Age society to a Christian society acquainted with Latin, and perhaps even Greek letters, the last and strangest conquest of Imperial Rome.

CHAPTER II

The Monasteries

IF ROMAN CIVILIZATION began slowly and by degrees to penetrate and modify Irish culture through the mission of St Patrick, the Christian reaction against pagan Rome had a much more immediate and dramatic effect on Ireland in the early sixth century. Christians, weary of the delights and fearful of the temptations of such rich cities as Alexandria, had flocked out to make populous the desert valleys and barren mountains of Egypt in the fourth and fifth centuries when, following the example of Paul, Anthony, and Pachomius, they became hermits or monks and sought spiritual perfection in solitude, in penance, and in fasting. The example of the Thebaid was widely imitated in the ancient world. St Honoratus, a noble-man of northern Gaul, who abandoned the world in this way, founded a monastery, on the little island of Lérins, near Cannes, which became one of the great centres of the fifth-century Church in France. St Patrick may have spent some time there; at any rate Lérins certainly had British connexions, and monasticism, presumably of the Egyptian type, appeared in western Britain in the fifth century.

Ireland, temporarily cut off from the centres of Christendom by the barbarian invasions, came almost wholly under the influence of the western British Church towards the end of the fifth century. British missionaries laboured in Ireland and many Irishmen went to study in Britain, especially in the monasteries of Candida Casa (Whithorn) in Galloway, and Mynyw (St Davids) in Wales. In the early years of the sixth century these men returned to Ireland and, in emulation of their teachers in

Fig. 11

49

religion, went in search of secluded places, remote from the affairs of the world, to build their cells and make their souls with prayer and fasting. Like the Egyptians, the Irish then flocked to the cells of the founders and made populous the desert places with the huts of monks and hermits.

The tendency towards monasticism already existed in Ireland; as we have previously observed, the ecclesiastical organization imported from the Roman provinces could only with difficulty be accommodated in Irish conditions, and the Irish social system with its emphasis on kinship and personal rule readily received the concept of the monastic family with its abbot. Armagh, the primatial see, seems to have become monastic by the end of the fifth century, and St Brigid had founded her great community for monks and nuns at Kildare. The old sea-route to western France and the Mediterranean—the route of the wine-trade—almost certainly remained open in some degree in spite of the barbarians and it seems most likely that there were some direct contacts between Ireland and Egypt. But with the return of St Enda from Candida Casa to found a monastery on the Aran Islands where he and his companions followed a rule of great severity, a revolution in the character of the Irish Church began. Early in the sixth century also, St Finnian, under the influence of Cadoc of Llancarvan, in south Wales, transformed the Patrician church of Clonard into a monastery which rapidly acquired great renown.

Figs. 6, 7

Monastic foundations followed in every corner of Ireland; Seir, Clonmacnoise, Derry, Durrow, Bangor, Nendrum,

Plate 12

Glendalough, and many more.

The ecclesiastical organization established by Patrick withered away in the sixth century. The administrative unit was no longer territorial, no longer the diocese but the monastic *familia* or the *paruchia*, the scattered monasteries which followed the rule of a single founder. As a corollary, bishops ceased to have an administrative function, although this may be partly

Tory
Fahan
Derry
Raphoe
Bangor
Nendrum
Downpatrick
Armagh
Inishmurray
Devinish
Inishkea
Fenagh
Louth
Monasterboice
Mayo
Ardagh
Fore
Kells
Inishbofin
Inchcleraun
Duleek
Cong
Tuam
Inchbofin
Swords
Clonard
Finglas
Clonmacnoise
Durrow
Tallaght
Clonfert
Rahan
Aran
Lorrha
Monasterevin
Kildare
Kilmacduagh
Birr
Kilfenora
Seir Kieran
Glendalough
Dysert
Inishcaltra
Roscrea
Castledermot
O'Dea
Kilalloe
Sletty
Scattery
Mungret
Liathmore
Mochoemóg
Ferns
Emly
St Mullins
Ardfert
Bri Gobann
Taghmon
Begerin
Lismore
Inisfallen
Ardmore
Sceilg
Mhichíl
Cloyne

Fig. 6. Map showing principal Irish monasteries.

due to the strictures on the bishops of his day of Gildas, who seems to have been the British teacher held in greatest regard by the Irish at this time. By the end of the sixth century the Irish Church had become a church of monks.

In two important respects Irish monasticism differed from its Egyptian prototype. Unlike the Desert Fathers, the Irish monks from the outset valued letters and learning, and, almost from its beginnings the Irish monastic movement was a missionary movement. The Irishman of the sixth century depended so much on his family group for his status, rights, privileges, and general well-being, that when he sought self-mortification, exile suggested itself to him as one of the greatest penances: to leave his own people and go to live among strangers or, as Adamnán puts it, to seek 'a solitude in the pathless sea'.[1] The words a later poet put in the mouth of St Columcille as he set sail from Ireland for Iona probably express his feelings well, and the feelings of many others who became exiles for Christ:

Fig. 7. The foundation of Clonmacnoise, from the carving on the Cross of the Scriptures, Clonmacnoise.

> There is a blue eye which will look back at Ireland;
> never more shall it see the men of Ireland nor her women.[2]

It was this desire for penitential exile rather than any evange-listic impulse which brought the Irish to the lands of the pagan Picts or the shores of Lake Constance.

MONASTIC BUILDINGS

Many of the great monasteries of Ireland have left little visible trace. Of Clonard, which numbered its monks, its scholars, and its students in thousands no faintest relic of church or cell is now to be seen. The literature, however, especially the lives of saints, gives abundant evidence of the character of the

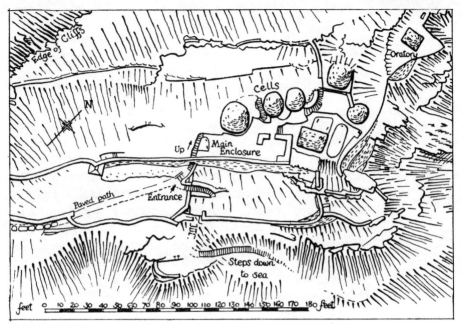

Fig. 8. Plan of the monastery of Sceilg Mhichíl.

monastery. The settlement was usually in a large rath or ring-fort, i.e. a circular enclosure bounded by a stone or earthen bank with a ditch outside. Within the enclosure the most important building was the church or oratory, a rectangular structure of oaken planks or of wattle and daub. In spite of its importance this building seems rarely to have been of even moderate size. The *cellae* or huts (usually of wickerwork) of the monks were dispersed about the enclosure, one or two monks usually, but sometimes more, to a cell. The other buildings of importance were the guest-house (*tech n-oíged*) and the refectory (*praindtech*), and if the monastery was of any importance there was also a school. This arrangement of the monastery in general

Fig. 8

53

resembled that of certain Egyptian ones, but some of the lives of the saints would seem to suggest that communities very like this in arrangement had previously existed as schools of the druids, some of whose functions (and especially that of education) were taken over by the monks. The life of the monastic community was devoted to prayer, penance, and learning, but there was also much work to be done—work that must, as the monasteries grew, have taken up an increasing proportion of the time of the communities. The monastic community was the nearest approach to a town in Early Christian Ireland; from an early stage a considerable degree of specialization will have become necessary. Buildings were required to house monks and students, books were needed for study, vessels for the altar, boats or other conveyances for transport, food for sustenance. All these were provided by the community itself, and in time the monastic workshops became the chief centres of craftsmanship in the country.

As a monastery grew in size the monks, instead of building a larger church, seem rather to have multiplied the number of small churches in the enclosure. These in most places were, no doubt, 'not of stone, but of hewn oak thatched with reeds after the Scots [i.e. Irish] manner',[3] as Bede describes them, and none of them have remained, nor has excavation yet revealed much concerning them. On the islands off the west coast, however, where some of the earliest seekers of solitude founded their monasteries, neither timber nor thatch was readily available, and buildings were constructed of stone. Eight miles out beyond the headlands of south-western Ireland the Great Skellig, a pyramid of bare rock, rises to a peak seven hundred feet above the Atlantic. Near the topmost crag the buildings of an early monastery, that of *Sceilg Mhichíl*, nestle on the terraced slope of a rock shelf behind dry-stone enclosure-walls which rise from the brow of a five-hundred-foot precipice. The early buildings (there are also ruins of a later church) consist of

Plate 6

Fig. 8

six beehive cells and two little oratories. The cells are built in a straggling row against the final slope leading up to a ridge, and they face on to a narrow walled terrace. Each cell is roughly quadrangular on internal ground plan, but the walls assume a circular plan as they rise and curve inward to form the beehive roof. This roof is formed by corbelling; that is to say, each circular course of masonry is made of smaller diameter than the course below, so that the courses oversail slightly inward as they rise until finally the gap can be closed with a single stone. In spite of their primitive unmortared masonry, the cells are remarkably smoothly finished on the interior; they are provided with stone cupboards or ambries, are paved and properly drained, and even today remain weatherproof and snug. The oratories are also corbel/built, but these are rectangular on plan and the side walls curve back to a rounded ridge. The end walls are also battered back, so that the whole structure looks rather like an upturned boat. Both oratories and cells have narrow lintelled doorways with inward/sloping jambs, and the sole ornament consists of simple crosses incised on the under/side of some of the lintels and crude Latin crosses picked out in pieces of white quartz in the masonry of one of the oratories and one of the cells. There is a tiny grave plot with small rough slabs incised with crosses, and in the main enclosure there stand two tall slabs, roughly shaped to the outline of a cross and carved in low relief with a simple cruciform pattern. In every part of the Skellig where it was possible to do so (and in some where it seems impossible) stretches of retaining wall were built to hold pockets of soil. Only sea/pink and a few other hardy weeds grow on the rock today, but perhaps it was possible to persuade a few herbs to survive the salt atmosphere (in stormy weather the sea/spume drifts over the very peak). Goats also can live on the Skellig, and the cliffs abound in birds, including puffins and gannets. Fish, too, are plentiful in the seas around, so that life could, with some difficulty and

Plate 8

Plate 7

without luxury, be sustained. And although the lofty dwellings of the monks might seem a more suitable habitation for eagles than for men, the cliff-top site was surprisingly well-chosen, has a sunny aspect, and enjoys shelter even in rough weather. Like so many other sanctuaries in high places, the monastery was dedicated to St Michael the Archangel.

The monastery of *Sceilg Mhichíl* was in existence at the beginning of the ninth century. The date of its foundation is unknown. It is the best preserved of the Irish monasteries and is one of the most dramatic monuments of early Christianity in western Europe, but by the very extravagance of its situation it is not fully typical of the monastic communities of its day. On the island of Inishmurray, off the Sligo coast, there still stand the ruins of a massive enclosing wall, fifteen feet thick at the base and originally fifteen feet or more in height, enclosing an oval space, one hundred and seventy-five feet by one hundred and thirty-five feet internally at its maximum, within which are remains or traces of *clocháin* (beehive cells) and several small stone churches. In the Midlands there are the remains of great earthen banks, once the boundaries of more or less circular enclosures, at several monastic sites—Inchcleraun on an island in Lough Ree, Durrow, and Seir Kieran. The monastery of Nendrum, which has been excavated, was enclosed by a triple rampart. The remains of the monastic settlement at Glenda-lough, a long narrow valley among the Wicklow hills, provide an interesting illustration of the growth of a great monastery over the centuries. Glendalough was founded by St Kevin in the sixth century; because of the renown of his sanctity, the place after his death became a centre of pilgrimage and the monastery one of the principal ecclesiastical sites in the country. The earliest settlement seems to have been at the upper and less easily accessible end of the valley. The remains of a small mortar-built church, 'Temple-na-Skellig', stand on a narrow ledge at the foot of a cliff by the shore of a small lake. This is certainly later than the sixth century in date but seems to be the earliest structure now remaining. Near by are artificially made terraces with remains of at least one *clochán*. The later buildings are dispersed for a full mile down along the valley floor, with one group, including a Round Tower, forming what seems to be a secondary nucleus of the monastery (perhaps of the tenth century) just below the two lakes which give the valley its name. Here there are remains of an enclosure wall with an arched gateway. In the lower valley there are ruins of twelfth-century buildings. Although it is unlikely that all the parts of the monastery represented by these scattered remains were ever occupied at one and the same time, the settlement was clearly a large one; a city by comparison with contemporary secular settlements, so that the compiler of the Martyrology of Oenghus in the ninth century could write in his prologue: 'The cells that have been taken by pairs and trios; they are Romes with multi-tudes, with hundreds, with thousands.'[4]

Plate 12

The little churches that were built in the monasteries have no architectural pretensions, but, as Leask says, 'they have a special interest: they were evolved—unlike those of western Europe in the same period—in almost entire independence of Roman traditions of building'.[5] Two types of timber church are con-sistently described; a church of wickerwork or wattles, and a church of hewn timbers. None of either type still stands, nor have the traces of any been discovered by excavation, yet we have quite a good idea of what the early churches were like, since it seems that the first stone oratories preserved something of the form of their wooden prototypes.

Perhaps the boat-shaped oratories imitate in general outline the form of wattle structures, but since they are corbel-built of stone the peculiar difficulties of this type of construction must have had their own influence on the finished appearance of the building. The most perfect of these oratories still standing is that at Gallarus, Co. Kerry. This resembles in general form

Plate 11

the two little oratories on the Skellig already described, but is much more perfectly constructed. It is built of large wrought stones, carefully fitted together to give a small gabled structure —both gables lean back in a curved batter—whose cross, section is that of a pointed vault springing from ground level. The vault is corbelled, the bed-joints of the masonry sloping slightly downwards to the exterior to prevent water-penetration, and there is a thin slurry of lime-mortar in the core-work. In one gable is a doorway with sloping jambs and stone lintel, on the inside of which, over the lintel, are two projecting horizontal flags pierced with holes, probably to receive the tops of wooden door-posts. The east gable has a plain round-headed window widely splayed to the inside. The interior measures 15 feet 3 inches by 10 feet 2 inches. The weakness of corbel-vaulting on a rectangular plan is revealed about half-way along the building, where the vault has sagged. The date of this little building is not known; it is usually assumed to be at least as early as the eighth century but it may well be several centuries later.

Churches made of sawn planks were faithfully reproduced in mortared stone, and the several hundred small examples of these still to be seen in the country betray, in some features of their construction, their timber origin. Of these the most

Plate 9

interesting is the one on St MacDara's Island, in the Atlantic off the coast of County Galway. This little church—it measures 15 feet by 11 feet 4 inches internally—is a simple rectangular building constructed with thick walls of massive masonry with spall-packed joints. Mortar was probably used in the core-work but is not visible externally. The building, like other early churches, has a stone gabled roof of extremely steep pitch and of corbel construction, a west doorway with a massive stone lintel, and, again like most of the early churches, *antae*—projections of the side walls at the gable-ends. Here, however, there is an unusual feature; the *antae* continue up the gable-slope as a projecting barge. There is a further refinement—the stones of the roof along the verge are carved to provide a false coping, raised slightly above the general roof level. As Leask has pointed out, the steep stone roof, built of corbelling, could not have stood for long of itself; timber braces must have been provided. The roof has long since collapsed and neither gable apex remains, but among the fallen stones there is a butterfly-shaped carved finial which shows how the gables were finished

Fig. 9. The Temple from the Book of Kells; greatly simplified.

off. Such finials in stone are quite common. The whole structure is a petrified wooden construction. The finial is clearly derived from the crossing of barge-boards or rafters and is similar to the forms evolved, e.g. in the stave-churches of Scandinavia. The *antae*, carrying up into barges, recall, as has been suggested, 'elbow-cruck' construction in timber. The steep pitch, common to early Irish churches, is desirable for a shingled or thatched roof in the Irish climate, and would help also to minimize the thrust of the rafters on a timber-frame construction. Furthermore, there is some evidence to show that early Irish churches were governed on plan by a system of 'modules', such as is frequently developed in a tradition of timber-frame buildings. The dimensions prescribed for a *dairthech* (literally 'oak-house'—the name commonly applied to the early churches) were 15 feet by 10 feet, and a proportion of 1·5 to 1·0 may be observed in the internal plan of many of the stone buildings.

The literary evidence indicates that the timber oratories were constructed of jointed planks. Shingles of yew-wood, or thatch of reeds are mentioned. There is a famous seventh-century description (by Cogitosus) of the church of St Brigid's monastery at Kildare; a many-windowed building, divided by screens into three parts, ornamented with paintings and linen hangings and with an ornate door. Several of the tenth-century High Crosses have tops comprising carvings in solid stone of little wooden oratories with steep-pitched roofs, gable-finials, and roof-coverings of tiles or shingles. The same form is repeated in a few saints' 'tombs' (probably large reliquaries) of carved stone, the most perfect of which is in the graveyard at Clones, Co. Monaghan. The 'house-shaped' or 'tomb-shaped' metalwork reliquaries copy less exactly the form of a wooden church. And in the Book of Kells the painting of Solomon's Temple shows just such a little steep-pitched shingle-roofed church as must have been familiar to the artist.

Plate 56

Plate 29

Fig. 9

The stone roof of the church on St MacDara's Island is exceptional. Most of the simple stone churches, conservatively retaining the lintelled doorway with inclined jambs and the *antae* on the end walls, had roofs of timber, thatched, shingled, or tiled. Ornament, for most of our period, remained extremely simple. Sometimes a plain architrave, of single square moulding, was made around the doorway. More often a simple cross was incised or carved in low relief on the centre (occasionally on the soffit) of the lintel.

The difficult problem of roofing a rectangular church in stone by means of corbelling was solved in some few examples by inserting a propping semicircular vault (itself not usually constructed as a true arch) under the roof. Since it was unnecessary to have wholly solid masonry above this, a croft was thereby provided within the steep pitch of the roof. A few stone buildings—'St Columba's House' at Kells, Co. Meath, St Kevin's Church at Glendalough, and the chancel of St Flannan's Church at Killaloe, Co. Clare, for example—have such a two-storied structure. Hardly any of the stone churches still remaining in Ireland, however, can be dated with any certainty to the great period of monasticism; some, even of the most primitive form, are certainly much later; and they shed light on this period only insofar as they recall the features of the wooden buildings which, by all accounts, were then almost universal.

Plate 12

Besides churches and other buildings, stone monuments of a different sort stood in some of the monasteries. These were erect slabs or pillars which, in their purpose and in their ornament, show the blending of different traditions. From late pagan times—perhaps as early as the fourth century—until the seventh century, it had been the custom in parts of the country, especially the south-west, south, and east, to erect sepulchral or memorial stones inscribed in Irish, in a rune-like cipher based on the Roman alphabet, with a simple formula giving the name and descent of the dead man whom they commemorated. Basically, the script or cipher used, which is known as *Ogam*, consisted of series of strokes cut on either side of, or across, a stem line; in the stone monuments the stem is provided by a sharp arris or edge on the stone. These *ogam*-stones are most densely concentrated in the lands of the Dési of Munster; they occur too in the lands occupied by the Dési in Wales—where often a translation in Latin, and in Roman characters, appears together with the Irish—and also in the areas conquered by the

Fig. 10

Fig. 10. The Ogam
alphabet.

Fig. 5b

Irish from the Picts in Scotland. With the coming of Christianity *ogam* epigraphs seem to have come under some suspicion; sometimes the inscription was defaced, the name of the ancestor (which would often be the name of a pagan god), especially, being hacked away, or a cross superimposed on the inscription to 'Christianize' the monument. There is no doubt, however, that commemorative *ogams* continued to be set up in Christian times, and there is at least one example (from Church Island, Valentia, Co. Kerry) where an *ogam* inscription was superimposed on an earlier Christian cross. Ogam-stones are not usually associated with monastic sites.

But another type of sepulchral monument, which seems to have been common on early church or monastic sites, was derived from a late-Roman form of memorial widespread in Gaul and in parts of Britain. This consisted on the Continent of a rectangular slab bearing a Christian epitaph surmounted by the Chi-Rho monogram, sometimes enclosed in a circle; in Britain the form was somewhat cruder, a rough pillar or slab being used and a curious combination of Chi-Rho and Greek cross sometimes appearing. One result of the Gaulish and British influence on the development of the Irish Church was the appearance in Ireland of such monuments. On a mountain at Arraglen, Co. Kerry, there stands a pillar bearing on one side a Greek cross in a circle and on the other the Chi-Rho monogram with an *ogam* inscription: 'Ronan the priest son of Comgall'. Slabs and pillars with monograms, with Greek, Latin, or Maltese crosses, often with expanded termi-nals, and with swastikas, simple knots, or ornament employing the rather poor repertoire of curvilinear forms of the period, still stand in various parts of the country. These were not always simply sepulchral; an incised shaft of stone at Kilnassagart, Co. Armagh, marks the land given for a burial ground 'by Ternóc, son of Ciarán the Little, to St Peter', and the graves were arranged radially about it. It seems clear that the founders' grave in a monastery was sometimes marked in this manner by an incised slab which then, because of the reverence in which the monastic founders were held, became one of the most sacred spots in the enclosure, the goal of pilgrims.

From this, it seems a natural progression to have the symbol of the Christian faith raised up as the centre and mark of the monastery, even if there was not a founder's grave to justify it. At any rate a cross-inscribed slab or column is often the most prominent feature in an early monastery, and more elaborate slabs were attempted as time went by, with, instead of a simple cross, a crude incised representation of the Crucifixion, as on a slab on the island of Inishkea, Co. Mayo, or a full cruciform slab with a carved Crucifixion and other figures, as at Carn-donagh, Co. Donegal. Wooden crosses were also probably erected; some of the free-standing High Crosses carved in stone (especially at Iona) show signs of derivation from timber prototypes.

Although the earliest sepulchral monuments seem to have followed old traditions in being standing stones or pillars, later monastic graves were marked by recumbent slabs, incised usually with the name of the person commemorated, and often with crosses, cruciform patterns or other ornament. The usual formula of the inscription was simple—OROIT DO N . . . . . .; 'A PRAYER FOR N . . . . . .' Even the more elaborately ornamented grave-slabs remained roughly shaped flags, usually of laminated sandstone, with a smooth upper surface wholly covered with incised motifs; yet in this medium some of the most elegant and accomplished works of art of Early Christian Ireland were executed. The greatest collection of these grave-slabs is at Clonmacnoise, Co. Offaly, where more than five hundred fragments or complete monuments remain; there is another large collection at Gallen, Co. Offaly, but by far the most striking group is on the island of Inishcaltra, Co. Clare, where the small monastic graveyard has remained undisturbed, and

Plates 13, 14

the inscribed gravestones of the monks may be examined *in situ*. Recumbent grave-slabs with inscriptions in Irish are known from various periods from the seventh century to the twelfth, but the great period of the art seems to have been the tenth and early eleventh centuries.

The Irish monastery of the sixth or the seventh century, then, was not greatly imposing in appearance; a circular enclosure within which stood a few rectangular wooden buildings with thatched or shingled roofs, and a cluster of round wattle huts, with perhaps a tall roughly hewn slab of stone near the door of the church. Yet this was the milieu which produced that most remarkable spiritual, intellectual, and artistic movement of Dark Age Europe, the 'Celtic' Church.

LEARNING AND LITERATURE

The sanctity and Christian asceticism of many of the Irish monks of this period is not to be doubted. As 'pilgrims' or exiles from Ireland they were successful missionaries of the Christian faith because they were like St Aidan, of Iona and Lindisfarne, of whom Bede wrote: 'The highest recommendation of his teaching to all was that he and his followers lived as they taught. He never sought or cared for any worldly possessions, and loved to give away to the poor whatever he received from kings or wealthy folk.'[6] This seeking of the way of perfection according to Christian teaching was undoubtedly the impetus which produced the great expansion of Irish Christianity at the beginning of the seventh century, but incidentally, as it were, the monasteries of Ireland became centres not only of prayer and penance, but of learning. The learning was Latin: classical and late Roman. There is some evidence, but only a little, for the study of Greek, while the evidence for the study of the Latin authors is abundant. Let us take, for example, St Columbanus, who lived in Ireland until in middle age he went to found monasteries on the Continent; from his extant writings it seems that he was acquainted with the works of Virgil, Horace, Ovid, Prudentius, Juvenal, Eusebius, Jerome, Sedulius, Dracontius, Ausonius, Gildas, Fortunatus, Gregory the Great, and perhaps of Statius, Persius, Juvencus and Lucan, as well as with the Scriptures. He wrote an excellent Latin, both in prose and verse, and dealt confidently with questions of philosophy and theology. Columbanus was an exceptional man, but he was a product of the Irish schools of the sixth century. The same monastic schools attracted not only Irishmen but students from other lands in great numbers. The pages of Bede are full of references to such travellers to Ireland in search of learning, and he tells us: 'All these the Scots received kindly and cheerfully, giving them not only their board and their learning free but books also to learn in.'[7]

The scholarship of the monasteries, therefore, modest though it certainly was by comparison with the learning of later medieval Europe, was high by the standards of its time in the West. The students who were so willingly taught by the monks scratched their lessons on wax tablets with styli—two such tablets with verses of the Psalms are in the National Museum in Dublin—while more skilled scribes copied or illuminated manuscripts in the scriptorium. The greatest care and the greatest skill in illumination were devoted, as might be expected, to the transcribing of Gospel-books for use at the altar, but many other books besides the Gospels were copied or compiled by the monks. This work would have been of value to the historian even if it had been confined to Latin writings, for some of these—especially lives of saints and tracts on liturgy, astronomy, or natural history—are useful guides to the thought and custom of the time, but fortunately the monks at

Plate 32

an early date began also to write manuscripts in Irish. The very extensive literature in Old and Middle Irish that remains today has been transmitted through the scriptoria of the monasteries. It is almost certain that there was a separate, secular, manuscript tradition which was of particular im, portance in the recording of the laws, but virtually all the other known manuscripts are of monastic origin. Most of the surviving ones are comparatively late, but they embody older traditions and literature. The oldest literature, derived from the oral tradition of pagan times, of its nature contained a great deal of matter which was not to the liking of the monks. Censoring and alteration of texts have therefore suppressed some of the more openly heathen content, but the prestige of the old literature could prevail at times over pious disapproval. The scribe who, in the twelfth century, diligently copied out *Táin Bó Cuailgne*, the chief saga of the Irish, completed his task faithfully but added his own opinion at the end: 'But I, who have written this history, or rather fable, am doubtful about many things in this history or fable. For some of them are the figments of demons, some of them poetic imaginings, some true, some not, some for the delight of fools.'[8]

The scribe's work did not consist wholly of the copying of old tales. A lively literature in the vernacular flourished. Under the formal and metrical influence of Latin verse a new syllabic lyric poetry had come into being. The poet's was still one of the most honoured of trades and one which called for a long apprenticeship and initiation, and although this rigorous discipline led ultimately in the later Middle Ages to monoto, nous and uninspired praise,poetry, it produced at first many lyrics of remarkable freshness and originality. The monks who copied this mainly secular literature often themselves added a quatrain to the margin of a manuscript, often a little personal note to relieve the tedium of copying other men's words, as when the scribe writes at the top of a page of Cassiodorus on the Psalms: 'Pleasant is the glint of the sun today upon these margins, because it flickers so.'[9] And then there is the twelfth-century poem:

> My hand is weary with writing; my sharp great point is not thick; my slender-beaked pen juts forth a beetle-hued draught of bright blue ink.
>
> A steady stream of wisdom springs from my well-coloured neat fair hand; on the page it pours its draught of ink of the green-skinned holly.
>
> I send my little dripping pen unceasingly over an assemblage of books of great beauty, to enrich the possessions of men of art—whence my hand is weary with writing.[10]

Most often, however, the poems express a feeling we should not expect in European literature at this date—the love of nature:

> My tidings for you: the stag bells,
> Winter snows, summer is gone.
>
> Wind high and cold, low the sun,
> Short his course, sea running high.
>
> Deep-red the bracken, its shape all gone,
> The wild-goose has raised his wonted cry.
>
> Cold has caught the wings of birds;
> Season of ice—these are my tidings.[11]

So writes a ninth-century poet, and to illustrate a particular metre:

> The little bird which has whistled
> from the end of a bright-yellow bill;
> it utters a note above Belfast Loch—
> a blackbird from a yellow-heaped branch.[12]

There are many stories, anticipating the legends of St Francis, of the early saints' affection for animals. St Kevin would not disturb a bird that began to build a nest in his hand, and there is a story of a bird weeping and mourning for St Molua when he died, because 'he never killed any creature, little or big. And not more do men bewail him than the creatures. . . .'[13] These, of course, are but legends; nevertheless, they express an ideal which is in contrast to the barbarism of the age.

THE MISSIONARIES

Fig. 11

Some of the earliest poems are poems of exile. The same impulse that brought the Irish monks of the sixth century to lonely islands in the lakes or off the coasts of Ireland brought them also much farther afield, to Britain, to the Continent, to the Hebrides, Orkneys and Shetland, and even as far as Iceland, with the result that barely a century after the mission of St Patrick had come to Ireland, the Irish themselves became missionaries of the Gospel in pagan lands or propagators of an austere and enthusiastic faith in lands where Christianity had already become degraded and corrupt.

St Columcille, one of the greatest of the early monastic founders in Ireland, left his homeland in A.D. 563, with twelve disciples and set sail for the Irish kingdom of Dál Riata in Scotland. He founded a monastery on the island of Iona, off the west coast, which rapidly became not only the spiritual centre of Dál Riata and of the extensive group of Columban monasteries in the northern half of Ireland, but also the base whence the conversion of pagan Pictland was undertaken. Iona is of great importance in the history of early Christianity and art in Ireland and northern Britain. Early in the seventh

Fig. 11. Map showing ecclesiastical sites associated with the Irish, fifth–twelfth century.

century, after the death of Columcille, King Oswald of
Northumbria took refuge there for a time. When he returned
to his kingdom in A.D. 634 he asked the monks of Iona to
found a new monastery for the conversion of his people, and
St Aidan came with twelve companions in 635 and chose
another island site: Lindisfarne in the North Sea.

It was in Northumbria that the rapidly expanding Church
of the Celtic west came into conflict with the mission that had
been established by St Augustine in Kent in A.D. 597. St
Augustine's mission had been sent directly from Rome for the
conversion of the English, and was established at Canterbury,
but its success there was extremely limited, and the Roman
missionaries seem to have regarded without undue rejoicing
the rapid spread of Christianity in the north. They had no
difficulty in finding fault with the Irish Church, which had
been out of touch with Rome for a century. Since St Patrick's
time the astronomers and mathematicians of Alexandria had

reformed the system used for the calculation of movable feasts, and the new system had been adopted by Rome and the Universal Church. The Irish, however, unaware of these changes, were now celebrating Easter on different dates from the Church in Rome. In response to letters from Canterbury the bishops of southern Ireland held a meeting to discuss this question, but they expressed their independence by sending a mission to Rome to ascertain the facts. When the mission reported, after more than a year's journeying, the south of Ireland conformed to the new Roman custom, without more ado, in A.D. 632.

The north, however, the region of the Columban foundations, with its ecclesiastical colonies in Britain, adhered to the old system. When King Oswiu of Northumbria married a Kentish queen, who brought to his court her chaplain, a member of the Augustinian mission, the absurd situation arose that the king and his queen were celebrating Easter on different dates. For, as Bede tells us, 'Oswiu being brought up and baptized of the Scots, and skilful also of their tongue, thought the manner which they observed to be the best and most agreeable to truth.'[14] Oswiu called a meeting at Whitby in A.D. 664 to resolve the problem. The Roman view, expounded by Wilfrid of York, prevailed, but many of the monks of Lindisfarne stubbornly refused to submit to this judgment. The abbot and a number of the monks, both Irish and English, left the monastery and departed from Northumbria. But, as some of the English left, so some of the Irish remained, and in spite of the secession Lindisfarne remained under Irish influence for long after. And it was not the only Irish monastery in England; Glastonbury in Somerset, Malmesbury in Wiltshire, and Burgh Castle in Suffolk, were all important Irish or mainly Irish monastic settlements. But the coming of Theodore of Tarsus from Rome as archbishop of Canterbury in A.D. 669 and the subsequent work of Benedict Biscop in

Northumbria, gradually brought the north of England under Roman and Mediterranean influence.

Irish monks in great numbers also went to the Continent in the sixth century, to Gaul, the Rhineland, Switzerland, and even to Italy itself. Some were hermits, seeking no more than exile, solitude, and penance. St Gall thus established a cell in the Swiss mountains which after his death, because his reputation for sanctity had made it a place of pilgrimage, became the site of a great Benedictine monastery, not an Irish foundation but a house much visited by Irish pilgrims. Others were monastic founders, usually in countries which, though nominally Christian, had long lost the fervour and purity of doctrine of Apostolic days. The greatest of these founders of monasteries was St Columbanus, founder of Luxeuil, Bobbio, and many other houses. He too was involved in the Easter controversy on the Continent, and in his assurance of the superiority of the Irish tradition, religion, and ecclesiastical scholarship he spoke in terms which make him recognizably not only an Irishman, but an Irish churchman. His remarkable success in spreading and revivifying the Faith was due, like that of so many of his countrymen at the time, to the force of example. The Irish seem to have made converts almost without seeking them, mainly because they did not seek worldly goods or temporal power; they preached by their practice.

THE CÉLI DÉ

But the sixth century was the heroic age of Irish monasticism. A slow decline set in thereafter. On the Continent, the less ascetic but more reasonable, and above all more organized, order of the Benedictines came to take over the Irish monasteries one by one. In Northumbria Benedict Biscop's monasteries of Wearmouth and Jarrow, stone-built by Italian masons, took the place that the timber and wattle settlements of the Irish had occupied. In Ireland itself the decline took a slower but more familiar form. The sixth-century missionaries, according to almost universal testimony, had scrupled to accept gifts, but later the monks in Ireland began to acquire corporate wealth through donations of land and churches to their monasteries. The inevitable shift from spiritual fervour to temporal cupidity and ambition followed, and in the eighth century the annals record, for the first time, a battle between monasteries resulting from a dispute over land.

In reaction to this gradual corruption, however, a movement of spiritual reform began within the monasteries. The protagonists of the reform were known as the *Céli Dé* (servants of God). They laid great stress on the seeking of perfection in the monastic state, on meditation, and on the study and perfection of the Liturgy. Many among them were hermits or anchorites who moved out from the monasteries to solitary cells in lonely places, which are often marked today by the place-name element Desert- or Dysert-. The *Céli Dé* were especially active in the south and east, and their chief centres were the monasteries of Finglas and Tallaght—'the two eyes of Ireland' —both within a few miles of the present city of Dublin. This situation was unfortunate. Before the reform movement had had an opportunity to begin a new expansive phase of Irish monasticism, in the closing years of the eighth century the Viking raids from the sea, directed chiefly against the monasteries, began, and Tallaght and Finglas were among the first to be attacked. The monasteries were indeed to survive the Viking ordeal, but their great days had ended.

CHAPTER III

The Life of the People

THE SOCIAL SYSTEM

EARLY CHRISTIAN IRELAND was not, in the classical sense of the word, civilized, yet it would be too simple to write it off, as the Romans did, and after them the Anglo-Normans, as barbaric, or even savage. Irish society presented a contrast at almost every point to Imperial Roman society, although it had some things in common with early Greek and even more with primitive Roman society. There were no towns or cities, nor were there even villages of any size. There was no central government and no central administration of law, no Civil Service, no currency, no State. Yet these negatives are not in themselves a condemnation of Irish social institutions. The primary unit of society was not the individual citizen but the family, and public responsibility for individual acts rested not on the individual but on his family. Private property was held by this primary family group, known as the *derbfine*, comprising all those related to one another in the male line up to second cousins. A number of such family groups made up the *tuath* (tribe or petty kingdom) constituting the semi-independent political unit, and there were about a hundred *tuatha* in Ireland, grouped into seven over-kingdoms which in turn came under the general sovereignty of Cashel in the south or Tara in the north.

Public law in the modern sense hardly existed; yet the great number and extraordinary elaboration of the surviving law-tracts would suggest that the lives of the Early Christian Irish were governed in the minutest details by legal prescriptions and restrictions. In fact these law-tracts seem to have been

largely descriptive; an elaborate classification of what was forbidden or permitted by custom. Custom and conservative
tradition, acting within the boundaries of the *tuath*, were the
agencies of order. There were trained jurists who gave judgment according to traditional law when both parties to a dispute agreed to submit the case to this arbitrament. The customs
and traditions themselves were pagan, modified but not
radically changed by Christianity.

Society as described in the law-tracts was rigidly stratified
into grades or orders, each with its own privileges and duties.
In practice there were three main social classes; the land-
owning aristocracy (the warrior class); the serfs or commoners;
and the *aes dána*. The *aes dána* was a special class with special
and extraordinary privileges. It included the poets, the historians, the jurists, the physicians, and the skilled craftsmen.
These had a status not determined by their birth, and they were
traditionally held in such respect for their learning or their skill
that they were protected by legal custom even outside the
boundaries of their own *tuath* and thus had a much greater
freedom of movement than either of the other classes. For this
reason they played an important part in the maintenance of
unity of culture in Ireland and in the development of that
culture throughout the island.

After the coming of Christianity the clergy seem to have
inherited some of the privileges of the *aes dána* and to have taken
over some of the functions of the learned classes. There was also
some conflict between the churchmen and the custodians of
the old learning; for the old learning included the teaching and
practices of the druids and seers who played an important part
in pagan Irish society. Even in Christian times the respect paid
to the *file* or poet was mingled with awe and fear. There are
stories of an effort made in the sixth century to banish the poets
from Ireland because of their arrogance, their abuse of the
privilege of claiming hospitality, and their misuse of the greatly

feared satire. By then, however, most of the clergy were Irish, with an inherited respect for their native traditions, and the poets, it is told, were saved by the intercession of St Columcille. At all events, a fortunate compromise was reached between the native and imported traditions of learning, and the great fruit of that compromise is the remarkable vernacular literature of Early Christian Ireland.

THE PEOPLE

Besides being valuable for its own sake the early literature is an important source of information on the life of the people. The sagas, the historical tales, the lyrics, the laws, all contain casual references or elaborate set-pieces of description providing such information, but they are sources which must be used with caution; the conventions of classical rhetoric or of Celtic stylization lead often to descriptive or narrative writing that bears little or no relation to the realities of everyday life, especially the everyday life of the common people. Nonetheless, in so much written matter there is a great deal of evidence for the customs and practices of the Early Christian Irish. The independent testimony of archaeological excavation is available to provide a critical commentary on much of this evidence, but only the literature can give us any adequate idea of what sort of people the Irish were before the coming of the Normans, and what was their manner of thought.

Thus, the anatomist, reporting on the excavation of cemeteries, can tell us that before the Anglo-Norman invasion the people of Ireland had skulls not very differently shaped from those of the country's present population; the sagas and the lyrics tell us that fair skin, golden hair and blue eyes were admired as the ideal of beauty. But the ideal, of course, was not the norm. In a population of mixed blood there were many physical types. A twelfth-century text quotes the words of a man advising his son on the choice of a woman for marriage:

> Do not wed the slender short girl with curling hair; nor the stumpy stout girl; nor the weakly tall one; nor the black-haired ungovernable girl; nor the dun one with very yellow hair; nor the black-haired swarthy girl; nor the fair boisterous one; nor the slender prolific lascivious girl; nor the ill-spoken one of evil counsels.[1]

Similarly there was considerable variety of temperament, but some general characteristics may be attributed to the people as a whole: impetuosity, quarrelsomeness, headstrong pride, generosity, love of nature, and a powerful sense of kinship and family. All of these characteristics were not necessarily innate; some may have arisen from the social system. Generosity and hospitality were greatly necessary, at least before the monastic guest-houses were built, and therefore were among the most highly valued social virtues. Personal pride and pride of family were attributes that followed naturally from the primitive aristocratic concept of society. But there were some features of the character of the people which should probably be regarded as innately Irish, especially the love of intricacy of pattern in thought, literature and art, and the love of categories in thought. The making of categories and classifications seems to have become almost a vice of the learned class; they are endless in the laws, and Eriugena in his philosophical work could even discourse upon four different varieties of Nothing.

ECONOMY

This intricacy of expression, however, was achieved with no more than a few elements. Life in Early Christian Ireland was simple and rural. It was a land of cattle, and its economy was, to a remarkable degree, pastoral. There was no currency, and the basic units of value and exchange were the cow and the *cumal* (literally 'bondswoman'), which was worth four cows. Wealth was reckoned not so much in acres of land as in heads of cattle. Milk, butter, cheese, whey, curds, cream, buttermilk, lard were the main food of the people in summer; beef and, probably, porridge, in winter. Cattle-raiding—armed forays by a king or a chief with his followers into the territory of another, to drive off as much stock as they could round up— was so common a form of warfare that it must be regarded as no more than a violent and bloody sport, a test of manhood and aristocratic status, as much taken for granted as fox-hunting was until recent times.

The importance of cattle is amply demonstrated not only by the laws, the stories, and the annals, but also by the results of archaeological excavation. Vast quantities of animal bones were found on habitation sites at Lagore, Ballinderry, Carraig Aille, Cahercommaun, and elsewhere, the bones of oxen everywhere greatly predominating over all others. The breed was the common domesticated one (*Bos Longifrons*) with variations in detail distinguishing the types from which are descended the modern Kerry, Longhorn, Hereford, Shorthorn, and Aberdeen Angus breeds, though these modern cattle are in the main of greater size.

So clear is the stress on cows in the economy that it has sometimes been suggested that the Irish in our period were still nomads, moving 'themselves and their huts as the cows ate up the grass'. This view will not bear examination either by the historian or by the archaeologist. The Law of Status or Franchise, which dealt with the duties and privileges of the various grades of society, distinguishes no less than six grades of *bóaire* (literally, 'cow-lord'), and these included all the landholders or farmers who formed the approximate equivalent of the yeoman class in England. The functions of one of the middle grades of *bóaire*, the *mruigfer* ('landman'), are so described:

Why is he so called? From the number of his lands; he has the land of twenty-seven *cumals*. He is the *bóaire* (cow-lord) according to judgment, the *bóaire gensa*, with all the equip-ment of his house in their proper places: a cauldron with its spit and handles, a vat in which a measure of ale can be brewed, a cauldron for ordinary use, smaller vessels, including iron cups and kneading-troughs and mugs, so that he has not to borrow them, a washing trough and a washing vessel; tubs, candlesticks, knives for cutting rushes, ropes, an adze, an auger, a saw, a pair of shears, an axe; the tools for every season, every implement unborrowed; a whetstone, a bill-hook, a hatchet, spears for killing cattle; a fire always alight, a candle on the candlestick without fail, a complete plough with all its outfit. . . . There are two buckets in his house always: a bucket of milk and a bucket of ale. He is a man of three snouts: the snout of a boar in a ditch which cleaves dishonour in every season, the snout of a bacon-flitch on a hook, the snout of a plough under the surface of the ground, so that he is able to receive a king or bishop or learned man or judge from the road, against the arrival of every party of guests. He is a man who has three sacks in his house every season: a sack of malt, a sack of salt for the cutting up of joints of his cattle, a sack of charcoal for irons. He has seven houses, a kiln, a barn, a mill (his share therein so that he grinds for others), a house of twenty-seven feet, a pigsty, a calf-fold, a sheep-fold; twenty cows, two bulls, six oxen, twenty pigs, twenty sheep, four domestic boars, two brood-sows, a saddle-horse, an enamelled bridle. Sixteen sacks of seed (in the ground). He has a bronze cauldron into which a hog fits. He has pasture in which there are always sheep without (need to) change ground; he and his wife have four changes of clothes.[2]

The precise numbers, here stated, of the *mruigfer's* possessions need not be taken too seriously, but the law-tract gives at least an indication of what was considered to be appropriate to the household of a land-holder, neither of the highest nor of the lowest degree of his class, in the seventh century and it is clear that his economy was neither nomadic nor wholly pastoral. Archaeological research has added a good deal to, and sub-tracted something from, this picture of the well-to-do house-hold. The isolated farmsteads where the land-holding class of Early Christian Ireland dwelt are represented today chiefly   Plates 3, 15 by grass-grown earthworks which are commonly known as 'raths' or 'ring-forts', and it is estimated that as many as 30,000 of them still exist, in every part of the Irish countryside where there is land even moderately well suited for grazing or tillage. Some of them have been excavated.

DWELLINGS

The ring-fort was an enclosure, usually circular, within which stood one or more buildings. The enclosure was bounded by a high bank of earth, or earth-and-stone, with a fosse beyond. Sometimes additional protection was provided by timber palisades. In more elaborate examples the rampart-and-fosse protection is multiplied, as many as four ramparts, each with its outer fosse, sometimes being found. Since it is extremely rare to find a well within the enclosure, the defences of the ring-fort must have been intended to provide protection against wild animals, thieves, and perhaps sudden cattle-raids; they could not have withstood any determined military attack. Timber was by far the commonest building material, so that it is usually only by excavation that the outlines of the buildings within the enclosure can be traced. In some treeless and stony areas of the country, however, especially in the west, buildings of un-mortared stone were constructed and the circular enclosure itself was protected by a massive dry-stone wall, usually without an external fosse. These 'stone forts' are especially common in western County Kerry.

Fig. 12

It seems that the ring-fort has a considerable antiquity in Ireland and that some were built as early as the Bronze Age, but most of those excavated have been of our period. Many of them were occupied continuously for centuries, and an old poem on the ring-fort of Rathangan, reflects on the brevity of human life, contrasting it with the antiquity of the fort:

> The fort opposite the oak-wood
> Once it was Bruidge's, it was Cathal's,
> It was Aed's, it was Ailill's,
> It was Conaing's, it was Cuiline's
> And it was Maelduin's—
> The fort remains after each in his turn,
> And the kings asleep in the ground.[3]

Similar circular structures exist outside Ireland, and as a result of his findings in the excavation of Iron Age sites on the Isle of Man, and of the Early Christian ring-fort at Lissue, Co. Antrim in Ireland, a German scholar, Professor Bersu, has advanced the theory that the whole area of the ring-fort was roofed, the surrounding rampart being merely a protective abutment against the wall of the great round house where people and animals were warmly housed under the one roof. Such a view is not borne out by the evidence of other excavated Irish sites, which rather supports the abundant literary evidence bearing on the question. This has been collected by the Rev. Professor Shaw, and it is clear from the earliest texts that the term *ráth* originally meant the rampart-and-fosse defences; the

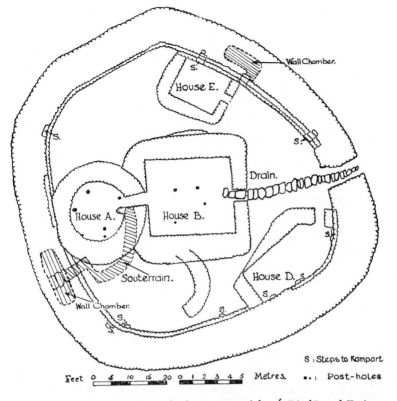

Fig. 12. *Plan of stone fort at Leacanabuaile, Co. Kerry (after Ó Ríordáin and Foy).*

word *liss* is used to describe what is clearly the open space within the enclosure, where trees grew, or bees were kept; while the word *tech* describes the house itself, which was 'made', in contrast to the *ráth* which was 'dug'; outside the enclosure was the *faitche*, a grassy open space at the approach to the dwelling.

This literary evidence is fully confirmed by the results of excavation, and the outlines of many buildings within the

81

ring-fort have been traced. Wattle-and-daub was probably the commonest constructional method employed in the building of houses but traces of structures as flimsy as this can be dis-covered only in favourable conditions. Portions of wattling were found in the lake-dwelling at Lagore, and remains of two wattle huts were found in a ring-fort at Knockfennel on the shore of Lough Gur, Co. Limerick. Both were circular; one had been destroyed by fire and the criss-cross wattles could be traced as a charcoal pattern in the red-burnt daub; the outline of the other, earlier, hut was revealed by a ring of tiny holes made by the ends of the wattles in the clay floor. Burnt outlines of wicker huts were also found at Grange and Ballingoola, Co. Limerick, but there was no evidence of date. At White Fort, Co. Down, there was another type of mud-walled house, square with rounded corners and paved within, and with four corner posts supporting the roof. A timber trapezoidal house at Craig Hill, Co. Antrim, was provided with a paved porch and a gutter for drainage and was accompanied by a souterrain. Where houses were wholly or partly of stone it is, of course, easier to recover information. In the stone fort at Leacanabuaile, Co. Kerry, a round house and a rectangular house of stone, with communicating doorway, stood near the centre of the enclosure, while subsidiary buildings stood against the rampart. The walls were corbelled but there were posts inside the houses which probably supported a thatched roof. At Ballyvourney, Co. Cork, a round hut was dry-built of stone on an un-enclosed site. The wall was constructed of two leaves or faces, the space between being filled with earth and rubble. Without mortar such a wall could have been carried to no great height, but it is probable that there was a lighter superstructure, perhaps of wattles or sods. At Carraig Aille, Co. Limerick, there were two strongly built stone forts on a hill-top, inhabited from about the eighth to the eleventh century. At the time of their building some need for defence must have existed; both were

Fig. 12

82

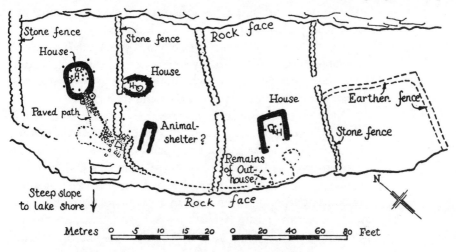

Fig. 13. Outline plan of 'The Spectacles', Lough Gur (after Ó Ríordáin).

provided with steps in the rampart and stout gates. Within the forts were remains of rectangular and sub-rectangular houses, but people continued to live there long after the ramparts had fallen into disuse; they had built one house partly over the destroyed fort wall and other rectangular houses with walled yards outside the fort.

Undoubtedly the Early Christian Irish did not all live in ring-forts; the rath would have been beyond the means or the social status of many of them; but unenclosed houses are, of their nature, not so easy to find. Another undefended settlement, not far from Carraig Aille, on the shore of Lough Gur, has, however, been excavated. Here, at a site marked on the Ordnance maps as 'The Spectacles' were several huts built on stone foundations, one round, one rectangular, one D-shaped, an animal-shelter, and some ancient fields. The round hut was about fifteen feet in internal diameter; there were posts inside the walls to support the roof, and there were two hearths, both

Fig. 13

near the wall and not, as is more usual, in the centre of the hut. A paved pathway approached the little house and formed a step at the entrance, where a porch was provided. The whole settlement was approached by rough steps in the rock, leading from the near-by lake which would have provided a convenient water-supply for the settlers and their cattle.

A two-roomed house on Beginish, Co. Kerry, formed part of a settlement of eight houses. Owing to its situation on a sandy islet the house had unusual features, some of which were also observed at Inishkea, Co. Mayo, another small island off the coast. At Beginish the builders had dug a circular pit about three feet deep in the sand, faced it with stone up to ground level, where the outside wall-face was begun, and then brought up both masonry faces and their boulder core-filling, together with a slight inward corbel. Radial roof timbers were supported in six downward-sloping joist-holes in the walls. A sloping way, flanked by retaining walls, gave access to the tunnel-like doorway which led through the seven-foot-thick masonry and was roofed with a series of stone lintels. The northern rectangular room, which was an addition, was less well built.

While most house-roofs seem to have been constructed of timber and thatch, hundreds of perforated slates, presumably from a roof, were found in a ring-fort at Ballycatteen, Co. Cork. Roofs of 'feathers' are sometimes mentioned in the lyrics, as in Cael's praise of Créide's house:

> Her bower at Loch Cuire is of silver and yellow gold,
> With pleasant ridged thatch of brown and scarlet-red
> feathers.[4]

This may perhaps be a poetical way of describing a roof of coloured slates or shingles.

The literature speaks frequently of a chief's *ráth* or fort being erected for greater security on an island in a lake but crannogs or lake-dwellings are much less numerous than ring-forts and are confined to a much more limited area, being most common in the region west and north-west of the Midlands, where small lakes are numerous. The crannog as a type is of great antiquity. Some of the excavated examples were built in the Bronze Age and rebuilt in the Early Christian period. The true crannog (the name derives from the Irish *crann*, a tree) is an artificial island constructed in a lake or bog, but occasionally a natural island was used and fortified; sometimes this can be demonstrated only by excavation. Like the ring-fort, the crannog was usually a single homestead with one or more houses, but its very situation implies a much more seriously defensive intent on the part of its builders (frequently the approach is by a winding under-water causeway), and the task of constructing an artificial island was much more formidable in terms of time and labour than that of making a fort. The large crannog at Lagore, Co. Meath, which has been excavated, was a royal site of some importance.

Plate 16

Although the use of large quantities of timber is a feature of the crannogs—hence their name—stone was also used and some examples have stone kerbs or breakwaters or encircling well-built walls. The normal method of construction was to build up the artificial island with layers of brushwood, peat, timber, clay, and stones, held in position by vertical piles, so that in course of excavation a crannog looks like a gigantic bird's nest.

At Ballinderry 1, a crannog of the tenth and eleventh centuries, a foundation platform was laid down when the lake was low and was held in position by large pegs. Outside this an irregular circle of light stakes was placed, smaller timbers were added, and over the whole foundation alternating layers of peat and brushwood were laid down, with quantities of animal bones and occasional slabs of stone. On this deposit laid timbers formed the base for the primary house, the floor of which was of wickerwork. A strong palisade surrounded the house, whose entrance was approached by a palisaded causeway. At a later stage in the occupation the surface of the crannog was raised and two houses were built near the edge, not centrally; later still, a layer of clay was laid down to bear the final house.

Large quantities of animal bones were used in the foundation at Lagore and the crannog was built up of brushwood, log platforms, and peat. Three successive palisades had been erected here, the earliest of piles, the next of oaken posts, and the last of tongued-and-grooved planks to form a continuous wooden wall around the site. It was clear that the carpenters were highly proficient in their craft. Evidence of this sort is more readily available from crannogs than from most sites; because of the wet conditions organic materials are often preserved and we have finds of wood, leather, and textiles from crannog excavations to supplement the record from drier sites where only the less perishable materials remain. At many sites old timbers were re-used in construction; a recently excavated crannog at Lough Faughan, Co. Down, has given further evidence of this practice.

Besides ordinary homesteads there were some forts of definitely military or defensive character, in use—if not actually built—at this period. The seat of the kings of Munster, the Rock of Cashel, rising dramatically from the Tipperary plain, seems always to have been a fortified site. The fine stone fort at Grianán Ailech, Co. Donegal, was the residence of the northern Uí Néill and is known to have been inhabited until the twelfth century A.D. This fort stands on a hill-top and is provided with battered walls, guard-chambers, terracing on the inside of the walls and steps to give access to this terracing and to the wall-top for purposes of defence. There is an outer fortification of hill-fort type, but since no excavation has been done at the site, it is not possible to say if this is contemporary

Plate 63

with the stone fort. Another structure at Staigue, Co. Kerry, is very like Grianán Ailech, but here there is a ditch outside the wall, a most unusual feature in a stone fort.

The stone fort at Cahercommaun, Co. Clare, inhabited in the eighth and ninth centuries, was well defended by three series of limestone walls, the inner fortress being massively built. The small irregular structures within, which were of very poor masonry, included a guard house and a sentry box as well as dwellings. And sometimes the ordinary ring fort had a strongly defended entrance. At Garranes, for example, an elaborate series of wooden gates defended the entrance, which was a narrow passage leading through the triple rampart and over the fosses. At Ballycatteen (provided with similar gates) and Letterkeen the sides of the entrance causeway were palisaded, and at Letterkeen this palisade continued around the fort outside the fosse.

Such elaborate fortresses are rare. A simpler refuge from sudden attack was provided in many ring forts: the souterrain, an underground passage or artificial cave, being tunnelled in clay or rock cut, sometimes lined with slabs and sometimes made from a combination of stone and timber. Some of the tunnels lead to underground bee hive chambers and the provision of concealed entrances and obstructions in the passage helped to make them secure hide outs, although habitation in them could not have been for long periods. In more peaceful times they were used for storage and some are so simple that this can have been their only use.

In Early Christian Ireland, as in Anglo Saxon England, there was one aspect of life, not touched on by the literature, which strikes the excavator as he recovers the evidence from a habitation site. King and churl alike seem to have tolerated extreme squalor in their homes. Food refuse and other rubbish was scattered and left to accumulate on the house floor until, seemingly to secure a level surface rather than to cover up the offensive mess, a new clay covering was laid over the trodden refuse, and the process began again. The reek of smoke which must have filled the dwelling from the central hearth was probably, in these circumstances, a blessing. The squalor, of course, is of advantage to the archaeologist, since the accumula-tions of refuse provide a fairly clear record of the animals that were kept or eaten.

HUSBANDRY AND FOOD

After cows, which were the main source of meat, pigs, sheep (including four-horned sheep), and goats were the commonest animals. Bones of horses, dogs, and cats occur also but in much smaller quantities. It is difficult to distinguish between dog and wolf, and information on ancient breeds of dog is inadequate; but at Lagore, as well as large animals (wolf-hounds or wolves) there were sheep-dogs, large terriers, spaniels, and lap-dogs. A small, active breed of domestic cat is known and these were a favourite theme of the artist; there are charming pictures of cats in the Book of Kells and the Stowe Missal and carvings on Muiredach's cross at Monasterboice and elsewhere. The poet and story-teller also were attracted by the habits of the cat; Pangur Bán, the scholar's cat is well-known:

> I and Pangur Bán my cat
> 'Tis a like task we are at
> Hunting mice is his delight
> Hunting words I sit all night.
>
> Oftentimes a mouse will stray
> In the hero Pangur's way;
> Oftentimes my keen thought set
> Takes a meaning in its net. . . .[5]

and there are many prose tales of the monks and their pet cats.

Most of the bones found on excavated sites were food refuse. The oxen were frequently pole-axed and the skulls were sometimes split lengthwise to extract the brain. Pig skulls were usually treated in this fashion and sheep skulls sometimes. It seems that horse was occasionally eaten, since at Ballinderry 2, horse-bones were split in a manner common among the refuse of

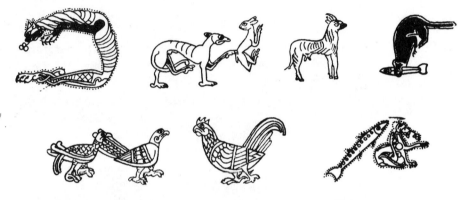

Fig. 14. Animals, from interlinear drawings in the Book of Kells: cat, hound and hare, goat, otter, domestic fowl, fish.

meals. A small proportion of other animal bones on the excavated sites—red-deer, otter, badger, hare, fox—gives evidence of hunting. Many carvings on the high crosses depict hunting scenes and the literature abounds with accounts of the chase. A twelfth-century poet praises a place for its good hunting:

> Your trout out from your banks
> Your wild swine in your wilderness
> The stags of your cliff fine for hunting
> Your dappled red-breasted fawns.[6]

Less sporting methods of procuring game were, however, practised, as is shown by the deer trap depicted on the Banagher cross-shaft.

Fig. 14

Domestic fowl were kept at many sites, but at Lagore and Lough Faughan it seems likely that these were fighting cocks rather than a source of food. Like the cats, the domestic fowl took the fancy of the manuscript illuminators and appear as some of the liveliest interlinear drawings in the Book of Kells. The majority of bird-bones found are of wild varieties—wild goose, wild duck, raven, heron, crane, black-headed gull, barnacle goose, Bewick's swan, whooper swan, cormorant, moor-hen, coot, owl, and many others. Although fish-bones, probably because of their perishability, are rare from the excavations—except from Beginish where numerous bones, mainly of the ballan wrasse, were found as well as net-sinkers and line-sinkers—fishing was practised to a considerable degree, as is clear from the literature, trout and salmon being particular favourites. Shellfish was eaten in quantity in areas where it was available and the gathering of a seaweed, dulse, is mentioned in some poems. At Beginish limpets and periwinkles were eaten and a small amount of oysters and scallops. At Caher-commaun the shells of mussels, cockles, and scallops were found although the sea is eight miles distant from the site. A large mound of periwinkle shells in the hut at Church Island indicates the partiality of its inhabitant for this food as well as the rather squalid character of his living habits.

Dairy produce, leather, and hides were plentiful by-products of the wealth of cattle. The number of bones from young calves found amongst the food refuse indicates that cattle were killed off in the autumn since winter fodder was scarce. In the laws flesh-meat is called 'winter food', and 'summer food' seems to be mainly dairy produce. A satirical tale of the twelfth century, *Aislinge Meic Con Glinne*, lists an abundance of foods, largely dairy produce or meat though there are many others besides.

*Fig. 15. A wooden churn from Lissue,
Co. Antrim. Height 21 in.*

In a parody on the genealogies, the abbot Manchin is addressed
in terms of food:

> Son of mead, son of juice, son of lard,
> Son of stirabout, son of pottage, son of fair radiant fruit,
> Son of smooth, clustering cream, son of buttermilk, son of
> curds,
> Son of beer, glory of liquors, son of pleasant bragget,
> Son of twisted leek, son of bacon, son of butter,
> Son of full-fat sausage.

and later, in a parody of the voyage tales, the travellers sail on a
lake of new milk:

> The fort we reached was fair, with earthworks of thick
> custard, beyond the lake. Its bridge was of butter, its wall
> of wheat, the palisade was of bacon.
>
> .   .   .   .
>
> Smooth pillars of old cheese, beams of juicy bacon, in due
> order, fine rafters of thick cream, with laths of curds sup-
> ported the house.[7]

Fig. 15

The rath at Lissue produced a well-made oaken staved churn and some of the lathe-turned wooden bowls from this site and the staved buckets, turned bowls, platters, strainers, and scoops from other crannogs may also have been used in the dairy.

Sheep provided not only food but clothing, and spindle-whorls of bone and stone are frequent among the finds from the habitation sites, while wooden objects from the crannogs formerly described as spindles have recently been recognized as hand-distaffs of Roman type. Lagore is the only site that produced textiles—all apparently made from the fleece of the sheep—as also fragments of cord and materials used in spinning.

As well as herding their cattle, the Early Christian husband-men tilled the lands adjoining their dwellings. From the laws one gathers that the seventh and eighth centuries were a time of considerable agricultural development when much of the fertile land began to be fenced off for the first time. The houses excavated at 'The Spectacles', Lough Gur, had a series of small fields adjoining, which may have been the tillage patches. That wheat, oats, and rye were grown is known from the literary evidence and from the finding of carbonized grains at Lough Faughan and wheaten straw at Lagore. Flax was cultivated too (Carraig Aille) and corn-drying kilns are known, while querns are numerous and a heavy mill-stone comes from Ballinderry 1. There are frequent references to mills in the Brehon laws and other texts—their erection seems to have been the task of specialized mill-wrights—and there is a well-known legend that Cormac Mac Airt introduced the first watermill into Ireland from across the sea through pity for his bonds-woman who, being pregnant, was weary turning the heavy quern. Coulters and plough shares, sickles, and bill-hooks have been found. Professor Duignan, who has summarized the archaeological and literary evidence for agriculture, says that

Fig. 13

Fig. 17

the coulter seems to belong to 'a low wheel-less, but heavy plough'.

Bee-keeping (an art possibly introduced, like the watermill, from Roman Britain) is frequently mentioned in the texts; and honey seems to have been a favourite food and may have been used in the manufacture of mead. Apples and nuts were plentiful, and wild berries and herbs were eaten. From the well-known ninth-century poem wherein the hermit praises his hermitage we have some idea of the possibilities of his meatless diet:

Produce of mountain ash, black sloes from a
dark blackthorn, berry foods bare fruits of a bare. . . .

A clutch of eggs, honey, mast and heath-pease
(sent by God), sweet apples, red cranberries, whortleberries.

Beer and herbs, a patch of strawberries (good to taste
in their plenty), haws, yew-berries, nut kernels.

A cup of excellent hazel mead, swiftly served;
brown acorns, manes of bramble with good blackberries.[8]

The literature mentions beer and mead frequently, wine less often; in the lives of the saints there are references to brewing. In a late twelfth-century poem from the Finn-cycle we find the mouth-watering description:

There is a vat there of princely enamel
into which flows the juices of pleasant malt,
and an apple-tree above the vat with
abundance of heavy fruit.[9]

Mountings from drinking-horns (and in one case the horn itself) looted from Ireland are of common occurrence in Viking graves in Norway and a few examples are known from Irish sites. A contemporary illustration of the type occurs on a Pictish slab at Invergowrie in Scotland.

A method of cooking by immersing hot stones or metal balls in water seems to have been widely practised. In the monas-teries water for washing was normally heated by the same method. For the cooking, however, we need not rely solely on the literature since there are numerous open-air cooking places or *fulachta fiadha* in existence throughout the countryside, a few of which have been excavated. These usually consist of a mound of burnt stones associated with a wooden trough— situated always where water is easily available from a stream. The dating evidence from these sites suggests an exceedingly long history from early in the Bronze Age until late medieval times. Professor O'Kelly, who has excavated several sites, has reconstructed one in all its detail and has carried out experi-ments in cooking meat by this method. He found that the contents of the trough—100 gallons—could be brought to the boil in thirty minutes, and afterwards a few stones added at intervals were all that was necessary to keep it boiling. A joint of meat was perfectly cooked and another was roasted in a stone-lined pit previously heated by building a fire within it; the meat was roasted mainly by the residual heat from the stone lining with the addition of an occasional heated stone. It seems likely that the *fulachta fiadha* were mainly used in connexion with hunting expeditions and a *fian-bhoth* or bothy is often mentioned as their accompaniment.

This was not the only method of cooking—roasting on a spit was practised and as in the Iron Age the great cauldron, large enough to hold 'a beef and a bacon hog', was the mark of the well-to-do household. These were of bronze or iron, and an iron link from Lissue may have been from a crane-chain for suspending an iron pot such as is used in many country districts to the present day.

A curious feature of nearly all the excavated Early Christian sites is the scarcity of pottery over most of the country. Some sites near the south coast have produced pottery of Roman or sub-Roman types. At Garranes, amphorae and fine red ware, very similar to those found at Tintagel and other Cornish sites, appear to be imports incidental to the wine trade and probably came from southern Gaul. The fine red ware occurs also at Garryduff, Ballycatteen and Dalkey Island, Co. Dublin. These imports seem to belong to the fifth and sixth centuries, and the trade which they indicate probably came to an end with the Arab conquest of Spain. Cooking-pots of a rougher kind occur at Garranes, Ballycatteen and Garryduff, Nendrum, and also at Lagore and Ballinderry. This type of pottery may have been first of all imported and then copied in Ireland.

Fig. 16. Pot of 'souterrain ware' from Lissue. Height 7½ in.

But altogether these fragments of pottery do not add up to very much and do not alter the surprising fact that sites such as Carraig Aille, 'The Spectacles' and Cahercommaun, where quantities of the ordinary equipment of the period were found —knives, pins, ornaments, and so forth—did not produce a fragment of that most durable of all household goods, pottery. One must assume that its place was taken by wooden vessels of the kind noted from the crannog sites, and also possibly by leather.

The picture in the north of the country is quite different. There, a hand-made, saucepan-shaped, flat-bottomed pottery, hard and well fired and sometimes having applied mouldings, is found on all the habitations of the period and also in many souterrains. Known as 'souterrain ware', it was well represented at the ninth–eleventh century site of Lissue and there as elsewhere almost every sherd showed incrustation of carbonized organic material both inside and out—indicating that these were

Fig. 16

cooking-pots. Sherds from Lough Faughan show similar blackening and almost all of them had chaff impressions on the base.

CRAFTS

The bigger farmsteads must have been largely self-sufficient, and many crafts were carried on within their enclosures. Carpentry of a very high standard was the rule, as we see from the crannogs. We have already noted the well-constructed plank palisade at Lagore, and the same site produced quantities of well-made lathe-turned objects—spindles, spindle-whorls, domestic vessels, and also carpenter's iron tools. The latter comprised a hammer, an adze, a saw, a draw-knife, a chisel, wedges, gouges, awls, and nails—all seemingly originally of Roman derivation. Dug-out canoes from several sites show the persistence of more primitive techniques. Apart from the more utilitarian pieces, decorative wood-carving may have been practised—chairs with carved animal heads are frequently depicted on the crosses and in the manuscripts.

Plate 35

Fig. 17

Evidence is abundant from almost every excavated site for the practice of metalworking. The techniques of the craftsmen are more fully discussed in Chapter IV, but here it should be noted that iron-working seems to have been carried out every-where—as is clear from the presence of slag and bloom on the sites. Crucibles for melting copper and bronze are fairly common and the site at Garranes produced fragments of several dozen at least. There are two main types: pyramidal and semi-spherical, each usually small in capacity. At Garranes, which seems indeed to have housed a colony of craftsmen, there is evidence also of glass-making and enamelling. Millefiori in process of manufacture was found there and some of the

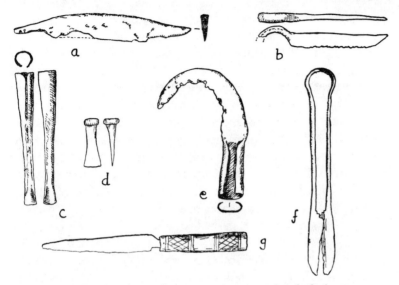

Fig. 17. Iron tools and implements from Lagore Crannog. a. draw-knife; b. saw; c. socketed gouge; d. wedge; e. bill-hook; f. shears; g. knife with decorated bone handle. Scale a-d ⅛ and e-g ¼.

crucibles were almost certainly for glass-making. At Lagore, enamel studs of the type used on the Westmeath brooch were made and a stud still encased in its mould was found, as well as millefiori rods. Besides the common 'trial-pieces' of bone or stone—the artist's preliminary sketches—other carved bones, possibly used as moulds in the *cire perdue* method of bronze-casting, were found at the same site.

COMMUNICATIONS AND TRANSPORT

All the evidence goes to show that each large farmstead provided most of its own requirements on the spot, and that the *tuath* was largely self-sufficient not only in law but also in economy. The ordinary layman must rarely have ventured beyond the boundary of his own *tuath*'s land, except when he accompanied his chief on a military foray or attended an assembly. Nevertheless, communications seem to have been fairly open. Clerics and 'professional' people could travel, apparently with ease; a provincial king, after his inauguration, made a circuit of his province to receive the submission of his sub-kings, claim his due tribute in cows and other goods from them, and grant them their *tuarasdal*, or 'honorarium', as his clients. An adequate network of roads and tracks must have existed. The five great roads leading to Tara were possibly constructed in imitation of Roman roads, but for information on these as on most ancient roadways we must depend on the rather scanty accounts in the literature. There are various names used for roads: *sét*, *rót*, *ramut*, *slige*, and *bóthar*. The *slige* was apparently an important road for the use of wheeled vehicles. The *ramut*, the avenue leading to the fort of a king, was kept clean by the people of his *tuath*, and there seems to have been a general obligation to keep clean a 'public' road, especially in winter, in time of horse-racing, or of war. Three cleansings are mentioned, 'of brushwood, of water, and of weeds',[10] which gives some indication of the nature of the roads. Wheeled vehicles were in fairly common use. The High Crosses bear many carvings of horse-drawn chariots or carts (different from the Iron Age war-chariot), and a wooden wheel-hub found in the crannog at Lough Faughan shows that they had spoked wheels, a fact also indicated by the carvings. In the early Life of St Brigid we are told that she attended an assembly (*oenach*), travelling in a chariot drawn by two horses. Such assemblies for the periodic transaction of public business continued from pagan times until the Viking period. A great assembly, of which traditions have survived in the early literature, was periodically held on the low hill of Uisnech, Co. Westmeath, on May-day; a large outcrop of rock on the side of the hill was regarded as the *umbilicus* of Ireland, the place where the provinces met. In historic times assemblies were held at *Taltiu* (Teltown, Co. Meath) and elsewhere.

The laws refer specifically to the horse as an animal for riding, whereas the plough seems to have been drawn by a team of oxen, usually four in number although the Irish word for a plough-team (*seisreach*) implies the use of six animals at one period.

The word *bóthar* is derived from the word *bó*—a cow—and, originally at any rate, meant a cattleway. The *bóthar* is amusingly described in *Cormac's Glossary*: 'two cows fit upon it, one lengthwise, the other sidewise, their calves and yearlings with them.'[11] A cutting across an old trackway on the Curragh of Kildare known as the 'Race of the Black Pig' revealed it to be a sunken way similar to cattleways in Wiltshire. Its date, however, is unknown. Apart from this, the only evidence that excavation has so far provided for this matter is of cause-ways or timber tracks which sometimes come to light in the bogs.

Overseas trade cannot have been very extensive, but wine, and perhaps other commodities were imported from France. Sea-crossings, for one reason or another, were of fairly common occurrence, as we have seen, and much internal travel must have been by water. Various types of boat were used. The laws employ several terms: *long* (from *navis longa*), *báirc*, and *curach*, the last being a light craft of hide-covered wickerwork whose canvas-covered equivalent is in use along the western seaboard to the present day. In the late Life of St Brendan it is told how the saint and his companions themselves constructed a hide-covered 'very light little boat, with a spine and ribs of pine, as the fashion is in those parts' (i.e. on the Kerry coast), while they had another, timber-built vessel made by shipwrights (*'fabri et artifices'*).[12] Two types of boat or ship are represented in the carvings on the High Crosses. Noah's Ark is several times depicted as a timber-built vessel with a very high prow and

Fig. 28a

stern and a central mast surmounted by a crow's nest. Such representations must, however, be interpreted with some caution; the sculptor may have been carving, not scenes that were familiar to him from everyday life, but those he knew from other, perhaps imported, works of art. An eleventh-century Byzantine ivory now in the Hermitage Museum in Leningrad, for example, has scenes showing the Fall, Noah's Ark, and Abraham's sacrifice, all three carvings being extremely close in detail to similar representations on the Irish crosses. The other type of boat depicted in stone-carving seems to be a clinker-built vessel propelled by a single bank of oars. A steersman, with a large steering oar, sits in the stern and faces the crew.

There are few references to bridges. Those that existed seem to have been comparatively flimsy timber structures (perhaps pontoons), easily destroyed, or else a sort of openwork cause-way—an elaborate form of stepping-stones. But the normal river-crossings were certainly the fords.

In general, however, the Irishman of Early Christian times lived within the boundaries of his *tuath*, and was born, lived, and died in one place, finding all the necessities and some of the luxuries of life in the produce of the one small district. In many ways he was better provided for than his peasant descendant in, say, the early nineteenth century. His diet, for example, although it lacked such a comparatively modern innovation as the potato, was probably more wholesome and more varied. Even if he was a slave he had the advantage of living in a society which had accepted the teachings of Christianity, and which, to some extent, recognized his rights as a man.

Fig. 18. Human figures from the Book of Kells.

DRESS

In such a society differences of rank and class were very real, but differences in living standards cannot have been very great. Dress was one of the recognized indexes of social status, but even in this matter there seems to have been a remarkable uniformity. For the dress of the period there is evidence in chance references in the literary tales, in the laws, and in depictions of human figures on the carved High Crosses, on metalwork, or in manuscripts. The common dress of the upper

Fig. 18

Plates 32–35, 51, 57, 64, 66, 71, 72

classes, for men, women, and children, consisted of two main garments, a linen tunic (*léine*), reaching to the knee or the calf, and a woollen four-cornered cloak (*brat*), worn over the *léine*, wrapped several times around the wearer, and fastened at the breast with a pin or brooch. Sometimes the *brat*, instead of being wrapped around the body, was allowed to trail freely behind, and a short cape-like cloak seems to have been worn for riding. A belt (*criss*) of wool or leather girded the *léine* at the waist and served also for carrying various small objects about the person. Shoes and sandals were worn, and sometimes a cloth about the neck. These garments are frequently referred to in the literature and may be seen depicted, e.g. the dress of King Diarmait in the carving on the Cross of the Scriptures at Clonmacnoise showing the foundation of the monastery, and in the figures of Cain and Abel on Muiredach's Cross at Monasterboice. They are probably best illustrated on Muiredach's Cross in the figure of Christ in the scene showing the arrest in the Garden of Gethsemane. Here a penannular brooch may clearly be seen fastening the *brat* at the breast. Here, too, as well as in the panel showing the Flight into Egypt on the High Cross at Durrow, where Joseph and Mary wear almost identical costume, an ornamented border to the *léine* is clearly indicated. This was the *corrthar*, border or fringe, and there is a description of girls weaving fringes of silver and golden thread. Embroidery is frequently mentioned in the texts. It seems that the *léine* was always white, or bright (*gel*: perhaps of unbleached linen), but that the *brat* was coloured, the most usual colours having been purple or crimson, and green, although black, yellow, grey, dun, variegated, and striped cloaks are also mentioned. Fragments of woollen textiles were found at the crannog of Lagore, most of them simple tabby weaves in which variations of texture were produced by variations of technique; though one was a twill or diagonal weave, and appeared to have been dyed with madder. Weaving-

Plate 32

Figs. 7, 28b

Plate 57

tablets for such textiles have recently been found in a crannog at Lough Gara. A black dye seems to have been made from blackberry juice:

> She has a vessel into which the juice of berries drips;
> in that juice her black shawl was washed,[13]

and a factory for extracting purple from the *purpura* shell was excavated by Dr Françoise Henry at Inishkea. It seems clear from the literature that dyeing was practised exclusively by women.

Tablet-woven braids found at Lagore may have been used as hem-borders but more probably were for girdles. Leather shoes, somewhat similar to Roman shoes, were found at Bally-catteen and Lissue, and belts of leather were also worn. Some of the numerous decorated bone combs found on excavated sites were probably worn as hair-ornaments. Glass bracelets, very similar to those of the late La Tène cultures, and beads of multicoloured glass of the same type as those associated with Dark Age Europe were also common. Men and women wore their hair long. A curious entry in the *Annals of Inisfallen* for the year 887, which seems to refer specifically to ecclesiastics, says:

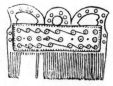

Fig. 19. A bone comb from Ballinderry bog. 2¼ in. wide.

> Anealoen the pilgrim came to Ireland, and the
> wearing of the hair long was abolished by him,
> and tonsures were accepted.

Ecclesiastics are mostly represented as clean-shaven; laymen, especially soldiers, are shown often with long drooping moustaches, and sometimes with forked pointed beards. Elaborate coiffures both of men and women are well illustrated on the eleventh-century shrine, the *Breac Maodhóg*. There were fops and dandies, who were vain of their appearance, especially of their hair, and employed dye, or artificial colouring of the

Fig. 20
Plate 66

eyelids. The three signs of a fop, according to the ninth-century 'Triads of Ireland', were:

> the track of his comb in his hair,
> the track of his teeth in his food,
> the track of his stick behind him.[14]

Most people probably used comparatively simple pins to fasten the *brat*; those who could afford it and were entitled to
Plates 19, 39, 48 such display wore elaborately ornamented brooches for the same purpose. The great law-tract known as the *Senchus Mór* laid it down that the silver brooch should be proportionate in size and value to the rank and dignity of the wearer.

In early times no costume other than the *brat*-and-*léine* is described in the texts, although there are indications that a slave could be distinguished by his dress. In the Viking Period another, quite different, costume was in use, and seems to have been worn by soldiers and persons of low degree. This con-
Plate 57 sisted of a jacket and trews; it is well illustrated in the panel showing the Arrest of Christ, on Muiredach's Cross, where the soldiers are so attired. It was the common dress of northern Europe—of Celtic-speaking as well as Germanic-speaking and east European peoples—whereas the tunic-and-cloak costume is a Mediterranean type, similar to that worn by Greeks and Romans.

At least two different forms of trousers are depicted: baggy
Fig. 18 breeches gathered in just below the knee, and long narrow trousers held by a strap which passed below the instep, like early nineteenth-century English costume. It is interesting to note that whereas a penannular brooch is used to fasten the *brat* of Christ in the Arrest scene on Muiredach's Cross, one of the trouser-clad soldiers wears a brooch of lozenge shape. This
Plate 49
Plate 35 may possibly be a representation of a Viking kite-shaped brooch, but a brooch of similar form is worn by the Virgin in one of the paintings of the early ninth-century Book of Kells.

In Viking times also new textiles came into use. Silk tunics and skin or leather cloaks are mentioned in late texts. By then, however, some changes were taking place in the economy of the country as a whole as a result of the establishment of sea-port towns engaged in oversea trade, so that new commodities became available from eastern or southern Europe.

WEAPONS

There is remarkably little information available about the weapons of the Irish before the Viking invasions. The draw-ings in manuscripts show that sword, spear, and a small round targe or shield were used, but very few weapons of this time have been found. Swords of late La Tène type, a short sub-Roman sword, and the Saxon scramasax were used. The *francesca*, or throwing-axe, also found its way to Ireland. But after the ninth century the Irish seemed to have adopted wholly the armament of the Vikings; even on the High Crosses of the early tenth century, soldiers are always shown carrying swords or spears of the type used by the Norse (but often imported by them from factories on the Continent). The battle-axe may always have been an Irish weapon, and heavy clubs are often mentioned and depicted (they seem to have been the usual weapon of the lower classes). There were specifically 'Irish' types (i.e. types used by the Norse in Ireland) of spear and shield-umbo in the ninth- and tenth-century armament of the Vikings. The Irish may have continued to use sling-stones in battle into Early Christian times—this method of fighting is often described in the early sagas. The bow and arrow were probably not widely used. There are depictions of bows and arrows on the High Crosses, but always in the hands of cen-taurs, which suggests that the carver was simply copying from imported art-objects this fabulous creature (a common item in

Plate 34

Plate 57

Continental Dark Age and Romanesque art, derived ulti‑
mately from eastern representations of mounted Sassanid
bowmen) and was not necessarily drawing on his own
experience. Iron arrow‑heads of the Viking period were, how‑
ever, found at Carraig Aille, and a long‑bow at Ballinderry
Crannog No. 1.

AMUSEMENTS

Fig. 20. A harper from a bronze relief on the Shrine of the Breac Maodhóg.

Figs. 20, 28d

The weapon commonly used in hunting was the spear, al‑
though it is possible that arrows (perhaps flint‑tipped) may
have been used to bring down birds. But the chase, next to
raiding, seems to have been the chief sport of the upper class,
and their principal quarries were the deer and the boar. They
had other amusements too, indoor and outdoor. Hurling, a
game which has survived and flourishes in Ireland at the
present day, plays an important part in the earliest stories.
Nowadays it bears a resemblance to hockey, but, like other
ball‑games, in its early form it seems to have had as its main
object the covering of distance with stick and ball against
opposition rather than the scoring of goals. Horse‑racing and
foot‑racing are often mentioned and are the subject of many
stories. Indoors, music and story‑telling were probably the
chief amusements. By far the most common instrument
represented in stone carving and metalwork is the harp, usually
a small instrument held in one hand and rested on the knee,
and plucked with the other hand. This undoubtedly was the
instrument that accompanied a recital before a company in the
house of a chief or king, and was therefore the instrument of
aristocratic households. Probably commoner among the people
were the simple reed pipes depicted in some carvings, or the
bagpipes which too are sometimes shown. Some form of

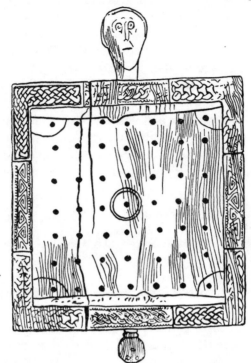

Fig. 21. Gaming-board of yew-wood from Ballinderry Crannog No. 1. Scale approx. ⅓.

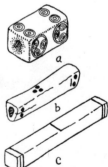

Fig. 22. Dice. a. (bone) from Lagore; b. (bone) from Ballinderry 2; c. (wood) from Ballinderry 2. Isometric projection. Lengths: a. 1⅜ in., b. 2 in., c. 3 in.

trumpet or horn is also depicted; this, however, probably had a function in the chase or in war, and was hardly a musical instrument in the strict sense.

Other indoor amusements were provided by board games. *Fidchell*, a 'battle game' which seems to have been similar to a Roman board game *ludus latrunculorum*, is often mentioned in the literature. A gaming-board of carved yew-wood was found at Ballinderry. This had a grid of small round holes to take the pegs of wooden playing-pieces, and it has been suggested by Hencken that it was for a game like Solitaire or Fox-and-Geese, though MacWhite has pointed out its suitability for an Irish game *Brandub* belonging to the *tablut* family of board games. From the style of the carved ornament, however, it

Fig. 22

seems likely that this gaming-board was made not in Ireland but on the Isle of Man. Bone dice were found at the crannogs of Lagore and Ballinderry 2. Those from Ballinderry were long dice of the type known from the British Iron Age, while the Lagore dice, although of an oblong form, were much squarer and wider and resembled those of the Roman period. Jugglers and buffoons are very often mentioned in the litera-ture, and Irish jugglers are occasionally heard of outside the country. Some of these, like poets and craftsmen, seem to have wandered freely, providing entertainment for their food and lodging.

STRENGTHS AND WEAKNESSES OF IRISH SOCIETY

King, poet, lawyer, monk, farmer, buffoon, slave, each had his fixed place in early Irish society. Each, if he was a freeman, had his status closely prescribed, defined by his 'honour-price', the value that was due for a wrong done to him. The boundaries of his world were small, although the custom of fosterage, whereby a boy was sent by his father to grow up in the house of another man, formed a network of relationships—often, as it seems, stronger than those of blood—which extended beyond the close limits of the family. Marriage, too, introduced some complexity into the property system, because the legally married woman had considerable standing and considerable rights; her property was her own. There were many women, however, without this standing. Concubinage persisted long into Christian times in Ireland, and marriage customs and relations, throughout the period discussed in this book, were one of the chief concerns of the Church. One of the few specific problems mentioned by St Patrick in his *Confessio* is that of the sad lot of slave-girls; more than two centuries later St

Adamnán secured a much-needed reform which put an end
to the bearing of arms by women in war. Marital morals were
among the questions that exercised the Church reformers of the
eleventh and twelfth centuries. But in particular the lot of
slaves, whether women or men, must often have been hard in
Early Christian Ireland, as in other ancient societies. The gang-
chains found at Lagore bear witness to that.

Slavery, like concubinage, was one of the features inherited
by the society of Christian Ireland from the Iron Age; it
persisted down to the twelfth century, a mark of the extreme
conservatism that was both a strength and a weakness of that
society.

Conservative though it was, Irish society had accepted
revolutionary changes in the fifth and sixth centuries, not only
the change in religion, with its profound effects on the whole
life of the country, but also, it would seem, a great many other
innovations, large and small, from the Roman world. The
study of pollen from Irish bogs has shown that, about the time
of the introduction of Christianity to the country, there was a
sudden change in the vegetation, suggesting that the new
agricultural methods, which had appeared in Britain in the
Early Iron Age with the introduction of the heavy plough,
were then first employed in Ireland. Many common items of
equipment used in Christian times were derived from Roman
models. Letters, learning, the rudimentary and speculative
science of the time, all came ultimately from the Mediterranean.
Ireland by degrees became culturally a province of Europe, but
a province where the outcome of the inter-relation of pre-
Roman and post-Roman civilization had not been prejudiced
by the superiority of Roman arms. Decentralized, politically
immature, Ireland at this time was yet able to achieve a unity
and a rapid development of culture and to produce a remarkable literature and a remarkable art.

CHAPTER IV

The Art of the Golden Age

THE SIXTH CENTURY had been the heroic age of the monasteries, the time of the great founders whose names were afterwards held in reverence by the Early Christian Irish, but it was not a time when art flourished. To judge by the surviving material remains, the monastic culture of the period, in rudeness and simplicity, reflected the monastic ideal, while the enamelled pins and zoomorphic brooches which were the products of the secular culture are a meagre and not remarkably accomplished art.

Fig. 3

But when the seventh century was well advanced, when the monasteries had grown in size and wealth, when the demand arose for liturgical vessels, for reliquaries, for Gospel-books fit to grace the altar, then suddenly a mature and masterly art-style, based on supreme excellence of craftsmanship, in book-painting, in metal- and enamel-working, and in stone-carving, came into being to meet the demand. It is its sudden appearance at the end of the seventh century that is most striking; at first sight there seems to be little to lead up to it; the Book of Durrow and the Ardagh Chalice have no worthy precedents. But a closer examination of the material shows that the ground had indeed been steadily prepared for this rapid flowering of art ever since the Patrician mission. To the small technical reper-toire of bronze-working and enamelling of the fifth-century artist new techniques had been steadily added, such as millefiori-manufacture, filigree-working, more elaborate methods of handling bronze and enamels. And with the rapid increase in intercourse between Ireland and Britain and Europe after the mid-sixth century, the Irish craftsmen became aware of the arts of their neighbours and were provided with an ever-increasing number of art-motifs to choose from.

Plate 22

The really fruitful contact was provided by the foundation of the monasteries of Iona and Lindisfarne, where the two eclectic eighth-century art-styles of Ireland and Northumbria originated, but it is probably wrong to try to distinguish too concisely between the Irish and the Northumbrian elements of this art in its early phases. In its origins the art was primarily Columban, generated in the monasteries of the *paruchia Columbae*, which were geographically scattered but were united in allegiance and communion. In the seventh century Durrow, in the middle of Ireland, was closer in many ways to Lindisfarne, on the far side of England, than to near-by Clonmacnoise.

The first major monument of the new style is the Book of Durrow (now in the library of Trinity College, Dublin), whose dating to the second half of the seventh century is generally accepted. It is the first elaborately ornamented manuscript, but its script, the layout of the ornament, and some other details show that it belongs in large part to a tradition already developed by the Irish scribes. What sorts of books were written or used in Ireland in the fifth century is unknown, although there must have been many manuscripts either brought in by the Christian missionaries or copied by their converts. The earliest surviving Irish manuscript is the book known as the '*Cathach* of St Columba', which may have been written as early as the sixth century, and this shows that the Irish had not only already developed a distinctive script— the 'Celtic' half-uncial—but that they had already begun to employ a tentative but distinctive ornament. Initials in the *Cathach*, which are drawn with the same red and brown inks as the script, are decorated, very simply, with weak scrolls like those that appear on the contemporary latchets, hand-pins, and brooches; many of the initial letters are outlined with red dots; and the enlarged initial is followed by several letters in gradually

Figs. 23b, 24a

Plate 18

Figs. 2, 3, 5

diminishing sizes of script leading into the main text. The *Codex Usserianus Primus*, of about the same date, has ornament confined to linear and dot patterns in the colophons, but the early seventh-century *Codex Ambrosianus D.23*, one of the Bobbio manuscripts, has a feature which sets it and the Irish books in general apart from the European illumination of the

Fig. 5a

time: the 'carpet-page', a page entirely devoted to ornament, here consisting of compass-drawn rosettes, disposed within a border of twists and crosses, and painted in red, dark green, yellow, and blue. Several features of the early Irish books, especially the dot-contouring (encountered in only one non-insular early book, the Vienna *Dioskorides*, an eastern manuscript) and the way in which the pages are gathered, show that the inspiration of the Irish scribes came in part from Coptic scriptoria. Some of the ornamental details, such as the Bobbio rosettes, were common motifs in western Europe, including

Figs. 23c, 23d

Ireland, at the time; others were derived from the patterns of Irish metalwork.

The Book of Durrow belongs to this series, but in elaboration it goes far beyond anything that had preceded it. It is a small manuscript of the Gospels which was for long preserved in the Columban monastery of Durrow, Co. Offaly, but which was written, as is now fairly clear, in Northumbria. The text is a pure rendering of St Jerome's Vulgate, probably copied from one of the manuscripts brought back from Rome by Benedict Biscop. Irish Gospel-books then and later used the Old Latin version of the Gospels, often mixed with St Jerome's text. The script of the Book of Durrow has the neat elegance which was to be characteristic of Northumbrian work, but the painting was clearly done by an Irishman or one trained by the Irish; he has devoted an introductory page to each Gospel, depicting the symbol of the Evangelist, but the symbols ignore the order of the text and follow the order of the Gospels in the Old Latin version.

Fig. 23. Spiral patterns from Irish art. a. 'The Petrie Crown'; b. The Book of Durrow; c and d. Bronze mountings now at St Germain; e. the Moylough Belt. Different scales.

The book is lavishly ornamented in four colours: brownish-black, vermilion, yellow, and green. It opens with a carpet-page, followed by a cruciform page with the symbols of the Evangelists in the four quadrants. Then come the Canon-tables of the Gospels, framed by narrow strips of interlacing or zigzags, and, at the beginning of each Gospel, a framed page on which the symbol of the Evangelist is painted against a background of bare vellum, and a carpet-page. There is a large ornamental initial at the beginning of each Gospel and there are other ornamental initials throughout the book.

The creatures serving as the Evangelists' symbols are stylized and rather childishly drawn, but the drawing of the other ornament shows great skill and assurance, matched by the artist's competence and restraint in the use of his colours; the brownish-black especially, forming outlines or backgrounds for the other hues, is handled to give an effect of richness.

The motifs used in the ornament show that the artist drew upon several widely different sources for his inspiration. Scrolls and spirals, directly derived from the tradition represented by some of the latchets and brooches and by the seventh-century hanging-bowls, abound. One whole page is devoted, within an interlaced frame, to 'hair-spring spirals'—tight outer coils of hair-fine lines which curve inward to fill up the void with smaller, sometimes ornithomorphic scrolls—linked by curved trumpet-shapes, whose terminals meet in small pointed ovoid motifs picked out in a contrasting colour. This is far more elaborate than anything in the earlier metalwork, and is like a revival of the richest La Tène style. A metalworking technique is also reflected in the stylized oblong body of the man who is the symbol of St Matthew; it has a polychrome chequer pattern directly copying millefiori work.

But it is the innovations which mark the Book of Durrow as the first major work of the new Vernacular style. Of these the chief is the profuse use of interlacing, based on a broad ribbon with a double-contoured margin and employed in running marginal designs or in all-over patterns with a framework of diagonal and circular knotwork. This particular broad-ribbon interlace was short-lived, but it appears on the approximately contemporary Durham Gospel-fragment (A11, 10), on the *Domnach Airgid*, a silver book-shrine, and on the slab-cross at Carndonagh and other stone slabs in north-western Ireland. It is derived certainly from Mediterranean, and almost certainly from Coptic, sources. The other chief innovation is animal-ornament, which appears on one carpet-page. Here the animal interlace is directly copied from the ornament of seventh-century Anglo-Saxon metalwork (Salin's Style II), but the composition, with the ribbon-like bodies looped in a rhythmic movement, departs from Anglo-Saxon usage.

Plate 5
Fig. 23b
Figs. 4b, 5d

Fig. 24a

The Book of Durrow was probably written about the time that Colman and his monks departed from Lindisfarne, after Whitby. It displays the three elements which went to the making of Irish eighth-century art: Coptic, Anglo-Saxon, and native Irish; yet it stands somewhat apart from the main stream of Irish art, simply because the borrowed elements had not been absorbed into the Irish tradition.[1] Some of the manuscripts most intimately related in detail to the Book of Durrow —the Durham Gospel-fragment, the Cuthbert Gospels at Vienna, and the manuscripts of the Echternach group—are English, but of the Northumbrian tradition whose sources are Irish rather than Mediterranean. In the large sumptuously illuminated manuscript known as the Lindisfarne Gospels, written by Eadfrith who was bishop of Lindisfarne from 698 to 721, the ornamental scheme is on the whole that of the Book of Durrow but the ornament in detail is considerably different. The metalwork spirals are still there but are combined with the animal-ornament and interlacing which had been kept separate in the Book of Durrow; and the broad bands of the Durrow interlace have given way to a thread-like fineness, while the animals have lost their amorphous Germanic character and have become integrated four-legged beasts, with dog-like heads and spiral-marked joints, caught in the interlacing of their own lappets, tails, and tongues, or long-beaked birds incongruously imitating the Mediterranean vine-scroll. The enlarged initials, the elaborate Chi-Rho monogram, and the dot-contouring of the Irish tradition are all there as well as the spirals, but there are other features derived from the *Codex Amiatinus* or from Italian manuscripts: architectural, arcaded Canon-tables, and naturalistic portraits of the Evangelists.

Fig. 24e–g

METALWORK

Plate 22

Plate 19

Fig. 31

Plates 20, 21

Plate 29

The clearest indications of what was distinctively Irish in the art of the time are given by the metalwork, so much of which remains in spite of centuries of plundering by the Vikings that it must have been produced in great quantities in the eighth and early ninth centuries. Very few vessels or fittings for the altar now remain, and the work of the eighth-century metal-workers is represented on the whole by secular pieces (brooches and pins), by fragments of mutilated objects, often difficult to identify, found in Viking graves, or by reliquaries. The number and variety of the reliquaries, testifying to the veneration in which the relics of the monastic founders were then held, is one of the most interesting features of the Irish Church. The wooden staff of an early saint was enshrined in bronze, pro-ducing the characteristic Irish crosier of walking-stick shape, with the crook ending in a straight drop; his iron hand-bell, shaped like the cow-bells still used in many parts of Europe, had a rich case made for it; his book, or a book attributed to him, had a metal shrine provided; even his belt was enshrined in an articulated metal casing; in later times shrines were shaped for the carefully preserved hands or arms of saints, and there is a shrine to receive a shoe. There are a few fragments of early crosier-shrines and one or two parts of book-shrines, but the reliquaries that have best survived from this early period are the 'house-shaped' shrines, small caskets constructed in the form of gabled or hipped-roofed buildings.

In the absence of independent dating evidence from Ireland, the chronology of the development of Irish metalworking at this period is supplied by the evidence of dated Viking graves in Norway which contain looted Irish objects. Three broad phases can be distinguished in the metalwork, corresponding very roughly to the first and second halves of the eighth century

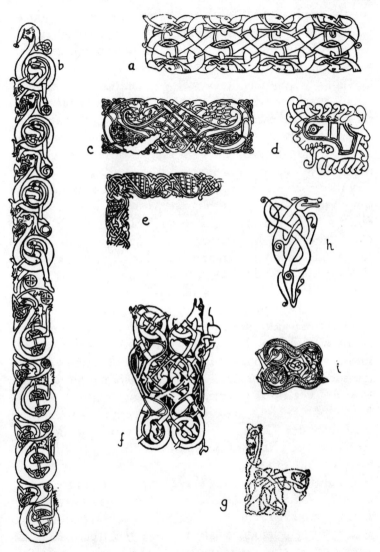

Fig. 24. *Examples of Irish animal-ornament. a. The Book of Durrow; b, c and d. The Book of Kells; e, f and g. The Lindisfarne Gospels; h and i. The Tara brooch. Different scales.*

and the first half of the ninth century respectively. In all three phases most of the ornamental metalwork is in cast bronze. At the very beginning of this period, in the seventh century, enamel and millefiori were the principal enrichments applied to the objects, and the ornament was comparatively simple: scrolls, spirals, or whorl designs showing as reserve bronze on the surface of red enamel, or little tablets of millefiori, floating in the enamel, giving a rather crude ornament. Sometime in the seventh century the enamellers learned to use colours other than red—yellow was usually employed in the earliest work—and they then used the reserve bronze to separate the colours, but simplified the patterns, setting the enamels either in plain oblongs or in interlocking L- and T-shaped panels. Such

Fig. 4c, 4e

panels are used on the house-shaped Copenhagen shrine (with garnet inlays), on the anthropomorphic escutcheons of the Oseberg bucket and the Myklebostad hanging-bowl (resembling the Matthew symbol in the Book of Durrow), on the handles of the Ardagh Chalice, and on the Moylough and

Plate 20

Lough Gara belt-buckles—frequently in conjunction with tablets of millefiori. This was one of the late seventh-century methods of decoration, but it was far more common to cover the surface of the bronze with engraved ornament, without enamels. The usual patterns were systems of trumpet-spirals similar to those of the Book of Durrow, but the bird-scrolls of the Lindisfarne Gospels are employed in very light engraving on the bronze plating of buckets from Birka in Sweden and from several Norwegian sites.

A rather deeper engraving was attempted early in the eighth century, producing a false relief, and the Irish metalworker learned, probably from the Anglo-Saxons, the technique of wax-casting to produce false-relief of the type known as

Plate 23

Kerbschnitt, or chip-carving, which is characterized by faceted and V-shaped cuts. The spiral-ornamented Copenhagen crosier-fragment is probably an early example of this technique.

In the later eighth century, casting was developed to give forms in very high relief or in the round, and the trumpet-shapes of the spiral patterns provided a medium for experiment, being zoomorphized into serpents or fabulous creatures (sometimes with human heads), who lift themselves clear of the bronze ground. Two of the most interesting examples of this fashion are a crosier recently found at Ekerø in Sweden and a pair of large bronze objects in the museum at St Germain, which have recently been shown to be, almost certainly, finials from an unusually large house-shaped shrine. Finally, about the end of the eighth century these experiments in elaborate bold-relief carving were abandoned, as were the trumpet-spirals, and the ninth-century style relied on rather monotonous rectilinear interlace in the *Kerbschnitt* technique. Animal-interlace is common on the eighth-century bronze-work. In the lightly engraved work of the beginning of the century it still seems to be partly influenced by the Durrow and Lindisfarne styles. The Lindisfarne bird makes a few rare appearances and the animals which accompany it on the terminals of the Bergøy brooch have some traces of the Germanic ribbon-animals. But a characteristically Irish animal, stylized, caught in the twinings of its own extremities, but preserving its integrity and natural features in head, eyes with pupils, teeth, paws, and claws, soon appears in the Irish metalwork. It is usually given rolled-back jaws, a crest-spiral and joint-spirals, and a hatched ornament of the body. It is alien to Germanic art but is probably derived, as Åberg suggests, from a naturalistic art—from an Oriental or Classical bounding beast of prey.

Plates 24, 25

The human figure, too, is sometimes represented in the metalwork, again in a stylized manner. The artists were not concerned with naturalism, and often one or two recognizable stylized features serve to indicate that a man is being portrayed. The head and the simply sketched legs are sufficient in the anthropomorphic escutcheons of the Myklebostad bowl where the bodies are simply enamelled rectangles. The most elaborate figure-composition in the metalwork of this time is an open-work plaque (probably a book-mounting) of the mid-eighth century, from Athlone, Co. Westmeath. It depicts the Crucifixion. The five figures all have enlarged heads, stare straight out at the observer, and are not to the same scale, while spiral and other ornament is distributed indiscriminately on the clothing, on the cross, and on the angels' wings.

But it is in the ornament of the more elaborate brooches that the heights of skill of which the Irish craftsmen were capable are first revealed. The old type of zoomorphic penannular brooch went out of fashion in the eighth century and a new form, based on the old, came into use. The general shape of the old was retained but the enlarged terminals were closed up and became one piece (a reminiscence of the gap being preserved in the disposition of the ornament), or were joined together by small strips of metal, so that the brooch became fully annular. Where the terminals are joined by a few narrow bridges of metal there is frequently an ornament on each consisting of a large circular setting in a trilobate panel. Side by side with the annular brooches the true penannulars continued to be made; the terminals, however, retained no vestige of their original zoomorphic form but occur in a variety of shapes, circular (as in a brooch depicted on one of the carved stone figures at White Island, Co. Fermanagh), lozenge-shaped, or more elaborately fashioned, as on the Kilmainham brooch. These styles continued throughout the eighth and into the ninth century, until the fully penannular form returned to fashion again in a late series of silver brooches.

On these fashionable ornaments techniques appear which originated in imitation of Anglo-Saxon work, but both in technique and in style the Irish workers soon parted from their models. The enamellers used glass or partly enamelled studs in imitation of Anglo-Saxon garnet and polychrome cloisonné

inlays; there are inlays of red glass, for example, on the Kilmainham brooch. But true cloisonné work was not done in
Ireland. Instead, glass studs were made with an angular metal
grille set in the surface, or with a surface marked with grooves
that were filled with enamels of a contrasting colour; or discs
of champlevé enamel in two colours were divided by angular
and fret-patterns derived from Anglo-Saxon cloisonné work.
There are such discs and studs on a brooch from Co. West-   Plates 19, 24
meath in the British Museum, on the Tara and Killamery and
one of the Ardagh brooches, on the Ardagh Chalice and on   Plates 22, 27
the Moylough and Lough Gara belt-buckles, while a glass   Plates 20, 21
stud of the same type was found at Lagore, still in the clay
mould in which it had been made. Filigree, too, came into use Plates 19, 24–27
in Ireland at about this time. There are earlier examples, on the
Newgrange finger-ring, probably an import, and on the tiny
gold bird from Garryduff. Again, it seems that the Irish gold- Plate 17
smiths borrowed from the Anglo-Saxons, whose skill in this
technique they soon exceeded. They first imitated the Anglo-
Saxon filigree by twisting two very fine gold wires into a cord,
shaping this to a pattern, and then soldering it to a metal background. Little pseudo-cloisons made of thin sheets of gold set
on edge and soldered into position show this type of filigree
work on the terminals of the Kilmainham brooch and again
on a gold ornament from Lagore. The filigree patterns are
usually simple spirals but sometimes an animal, with granu-
lated body, is outlined in this way.

A most interesting variety of techniques may be seen on the
mountings of a group of small lead weights from the Viking
cemetery at Islandbridge, outside Dublin. One has a gilt
bronze animal-head with blue enamel eyes and spirals in
nostrils and ears; a second, an inlay of copper and silver in a
zigzag pattern; a third, a gilt bronze plate with panels of
millefiori alternating with yellow enamel; a fourth, twisted blue
glass rods in a silver setting; a fifth, a cruciform pattern in red

enamel inlaid with wavy lines of silver, with key-patterns in red and green enamel in the four quadrants.

Most of the techniques described, and some others, are used with dazzling proficiency of craftsmanship on the two major achievements of the Irish metalworkers' art in the eighth century: the Tara brooch and the Ardagh Chalice. The brooch (found at Bettystown, Co. Meath, and having no connexion with Tara) is one of the earliest of the type in which the terminals have been brought together to form one solid piece, and is comparatively small. It is of silver gilt, with an extraordinarily elaborate and fine ornament on both front and back. The outer raised rim and the keystone-shaped pin-head curve off into cast reptile- or bird-heads, and the heavy rim frames dozens of panels filled with fine and elaborate gold filigreed animals, gold wire interlace and key-patterns, and dividing bands of amber panels punctuated by the large blue and red studs. There is a superabundance of minutely fine orna-ment; it crawls over all the surfaces of the back of the pin-head and the ring, where long panels of chip-carved trumpet-spirals alternate with panels of hatched and interlaced ribbon-animals or birds. The fine lines of the trumpet-spirals on the back of the united terminals are delicate copper relief showing against a wash of silver. In spite of the crowding of minute ornament into every available millimetre of space, the work is so assured, so perfectly executed, and so skilfully balanced that it is a triumphant *tour de force*.

The chalice is designed with much more restraint, but where there is ornament it is executed with a skill surpassing that of the work on the brooch. It was found, together with a smaller unornamented chalice and some brooches, buried in what had clearly been intended as a temporary hiding place at Ardagh, Co. Limerick. It is a large, heavy vessel of silver which could be lifted comfortably only by using both hands. The ornament, of gold, gilt-bronze, glass, and enamel, is confined to the

Plates 19, 24

Plates 22, 23, 25, 26, 27

handles, a band running around the cup below the rim, four isolated panels on the curve of the cup, the stem, a band around the flat part of the base, and the convex underside of the base immediately below the stem. The filigrees of the main orna/ mental band below the rim are elaborately constructed on an almost microscopic scale, built up in layers of beaded or twisted gold wires soldered on to a gold foil background in which the patterns have previously been marked in repoussé outline. The studs and some of the angular enamel panels seem to be divided by stepped or rectilinear grids which are actually grilles of silver set in the surface of the glaze; and sometimes red enamel is set in the surface of blue glass. Some of the studs have small circular central panels of gold granulation, and in some panels of the handles there is granulation in two planes; on tiny raised bosses and on their background. The raised borders of the main ornamental band are ring/punched, a sort of rustication to define the transition to the smooth silver surface of the cup. Under this band the names of the Twelve Apostles, in the elegant lettering of the Lindisfarne Gospels, are traced against a subdued background/band of punched dots. The stem is decorated with chip/carved ornament of beautiful precision. On the underside of the base there are panels of fine silver mesh, with a different pattern of weave in each panel. Other panels have little tablets of light blue glass through which a design in repoussé on gold foil can be dimly seen. This is the masterpiece of the eighth century, not only in the superb skills that went into its making, but in the unwonted restraint and sureness displayed in the placing of the ornament. If it has a fault it is in the general shape of the vessel which in its somewhat squat heaviness does not do justice to the brilliance of its ornament.

HIGH CROSSES

Plates 36–38

One of the strangest phenomena of the Irish art of this time is the translation of the fine patterns of the goldsmiths and bronzesmiths into carved sandstone. At Ahenny, Co. Tipperary, there stand two High Crosses displaying the engraved trumpet-patterns, the close-woven interlace, the fret-patterns, even the very ornamental bosses which should cover rivet-heads, and the heavy cylindrical angle-mouldings which should cover the junction of bronze plates, of metalwork. The form of the crosses is also of interest. They stand on heavy pyramidal bases, they have shafts and arms of oblong section, and a large heavy open ring marks the crossing of transom and shaft. No Crucifixion is depicted, nor is there any figure-carving save on the bases, where animals and trees, a hunting-scene, the funeral of a beheaded man, and groups of ecclesiastics are shown.

A detail of the funeral scene carved on the base of the north cross gives a clue to the origin of the form. Here an ecclesiastic is shown carrying a ringed cross in the procession. The late Professor Ó Ríordáin has pointed out that a heavy timber cross would, when carried about, impose a strain upon the joint at the crossing, which might be countered by fixing stays across the four angles, and that the most pleasing form to give these stays would be quadrants of a circle, so that they might form a ring at the cross-head. It would be fully in keeping with the customs of the time for processional crosses, or crosses intended to stand on the altar, to have an outer covering of ornamental metalwork, and it is just such metal-plated crosses, translated into stone, that we see at Ahenny. The custom of erecting monumental crosses at monastic sites was an insular peculiarity of the time. From the earliest period of Christianity in Ireland crosses had been engraved on standing stones, or carved on slabs to be set up in the monasteries as a symbol of the Faith.

Though some of the slabs, such as that at Carndonagh, had already assumed a cruciform shape, the Ahenny monuments are the earliest true High Crosses in Ireland, and they clearly owe their form to a tradition other than that of the slabs. From English evidence it is known that the Irish missionaries erected wooden crosses in Northumbria, planting them as symbols of Christianity in that pagan land, and preaching the Gospel from the foot of the cross. Crosses in stone were erected in

Fig. 25. A funeral, from a carving on the North Cross at Ahenny.

Northumbria in the early eighth century, but this was after the departure of the Irish, and the earliest of them are ornamented with a completely Mediterranean art, the art of the sixth-century ivory bishop's chair at Ravenna. However, on Iona—that all-important link in the art of the time between Ireland and Britain—there are stone crosses which, like those at Ahenny, have the bosses and motifs of the metalwork; at the same time, in the manner in which the stones that compose them are jointed together, they show the influence of timber prototypes. It has even been suggested that some timber was used in their construction and that they are now incomplete.

But there are no crosses of this type in the north of Ireland. The Ahenny monuments are part of a group of very limited

Fig. 27

distribution, at Kilkeeran, Kilree, Killamery, Lorrha, and a few other places in south Tipperary and south Kilkenny, at the foot of Slievenaman. They all have the same general character; figure carving, in the main, is confined to the bases, while the shafts, arms, and rings are ornamented with the patterns which are already familiar from the metalwork. A few other patterns also appear—a curious interlace of human bodies at Ahenny, for instance—and on the later examples one or two scenes from the Old Testament are to be seen on the arms, foreshadowing the later widespread development of the High Cross of Ireland.

THE LATER MANUSCRIPTS

The final major achievement of this intricate Irish art, like the first, was in manuscript illumination. Illumination had a very complex development in the eighth century, when intercourse between the scriptoria of Ireland, of Northumbria, of southern England, of Echternach, of Utrecht, of St Gall, of Bobbio, and many more places brought about a great interplay of diverse influences. The general tendency, so far as Irish work was concerned, was towards a steady increase in ornament—in enlargement of initials (and especially the Chi-Rho monogram), and in illustration of the text—and a considerable faithfulness to Coptic models. This development must largely be inferred from the distinctively Irish pages, due to Irish influence, that appear in some Northumbrian or Continental manuscripts; the Irish material itself is very fragmentary for the period. The manuscripts of the Echternach group, some of which, as has been noted, show traces of the animal-style of the Book of Durrow, also have many patterns whose counterparts are on Irish metalwork—the spirals of the Maihingen Gospel and the spirals and animals of the Thomas Evangeliar, for example. There are also traces of the influence of the Book of Lindisfarne, and these are very marked in some pages of the Lichfield Gospels, though this is otherwise very Irish in its style, especially in its lively animal-ornament and in the portraits of the Evangelists which anticipate those in the Book of Kells. Other styles besides those of Ireland and Northumbria appear in the manuscripts of this time: architectural details from the south, or foliage such as that which appears in the Book of Kells.

The St Gall Gospel-book, *Codex 51*, written by an Irishman (possibly in Switzerland) probably early in the second half of the eighth century, is richly ornamented and shows the full development of some features; the Chi-Rho, which has been steadily increasing in size and elaboration ever since the *Cathach*, is now simply the theme for an ornamental page. Most of the decoration consists of spirals and animal-interlacing, of the same type as those on the metalwork, but simpler, less lively, and with less of the balanced tension of the bronze-smith's art. Each Evangelist in his portrait stares rigidly full face and holds a book in his hands. The whole work is Plate 33 impressive, but is an example of a rather naïve, almost rustic art. And the same is true of the several ninth-century Irish manuscripts which have survived, including the very large Gospel-book painted with painstaking elaboration by Mac Regol of Birr in the first half of the century.

In contrast, the Book of Kells displays all the astonishing Plates 34, 35 exuberance and sophistication of the Ardagh Chalice. It is a large manuscript of the Four Gospels, probably written and illuminated in Iona in the opening years of the ninth century and brought from there in a still unfinished state when many of the monks fled from the monastery after the first Viking raids, taking the relics of St Columcille and other precious possessions to the new monastery of Kells, Co. Meath. The book opens with an elaborate cruciform page, which is followed by the Canons of Concordance of the Gospels, in arcaded frames, with the symbols of the Evangelists. The Gospels open each with an elaborate page for these symbols, followed by a portrait page. The initial pages of the Gospels are elaborately illuminated, and the Chi-Rho introducing the genealogy of Christ in the Gospel of St Matthew forms a

Plate 34

carpet-page in itself. All the initials of the genealogy are ornamented; ornamental, too, are the initials of paragraphs

Fig. 24b

throughout the book, consisting of interlaced men, animals, birds, or fantastic creatures. There are full-page illustrations to

Plate 35

the text: the Virgin and Child; the Arrest of Christ; the Temptation of Christ; in addition, there are several blank pages which were intended for further illustrations. Through-

Figs. 14, 18

out the text there are interlinear drawings of men and animals, everyday scenes, cats, mice, domestic fowl, inserted without relevance to the text itself. The ornament, in its fantastic complexity, in its profuseness, in its unfailing skill and energy, is quite astonishing. The trumpet-spiral ornament is lavish here as never before; the thousands of spirals within spirals, occasionally relieved by panels of interlacing, of the Chi-Rho page, are like a strange and infinitely complex universe in themselves. Other pages, devoted to illustrations, have wide-eyed, bearded Byzantine faces staring out from a mysterious world of

Figs. 24c, 24d

fabulous scenes and creatures, framed within borders which are covered with minutely intertwined ribbon-animals. The range of colours used is great—purples, blues, reds, yellows, and greens—and the use of the colours, especially the extensive use of purple, enhances the richness of the book's appearance.

The ornament of the Book of Kells draws upon the whole range of the Irish art-styles of the eighth century and also, to some extent, of the manuscript art of the Continent. A study of the Canon-tables has demonstrated that they are derived from a manuscript of the Ada School; the initials composed of intertwined animals are derived from Merovingian manuscripts, and the foliage—also found in the Leningrad Gospels—must also be derived from the Continent. The Northumbrian vine-scroll appears, and the influence of the Book of Lindisfarne is manifest. But the Book of Kells combines all of these into a whole which is often incoherent in general, but is as coherently detailed as life, with every minute cell of its organic structure carefully composed.

This extraordinary manuscript is difficult to approach or to judge as a work of art. Its mysterious motives are too remote from the twentieth century (although they form one of the minor obsessive themes of that latter-day example of Celtic concentration on intricate pattern, *Finnegans Wake*) and they achieve too fully the aims of an art which was non-classical, non-representational, non-humanistic, and which was destined to remain outside the main stream of European culture. But if the Book of Kells is to be marvelled at rather than enjoyed, it demonstrates, as does the Ardagh Chalice, that within the limits of their own purpose the Irish artists of the eighth century were able to achieve complete mastery over the medium they chose. Eighth-century Ireland was not civilized; it lacked the cities, coinage, institutions which the word connotes. But it was, in the sense in which Toynbee has so described it, a civilization, a society historically distinct; an abortive civilization, admittedly, but one which in the eighth century had achieved its first expansion of life and culture. Its art can never be fully understood now, but in it can be sensed that confidence in its own values which had earlier been expressed by St Columbanus when writing to Gregory the Great on the Paschal controversy: 'By our professors and the Old Irish savants and computists most skilled in making computations, Victorius not only was not accepted but was thought an object of derision or pity rather than a reliable scholar.'[2] And St Donatus, an Irishman who was bishop of

Fiesole in the ninth century, expressed the same feelings in a more positive fashion, in a Latin verse on Ireland in the Golden Age (in the Irish fashion, he adapted from a foreign model— from Virgil's lines on Italy in the second Georgic):

The noblest share of earth is the far western world
Whose name is written Scottia in the ancient books;
Rich in goods, in silver, jewels, cloth and gold,
Benign to the body, in air and mellow soil.
With honey and with milk flow Ireland's lovely plains,
With silk and arms, abundant fruit, with art and men.

No fury of bears is there, and the Irish land
Never has nurtured the savage seed of lions;
There no poison harms, no serpent glides in the grass,
No frog harshly sings his loud complaint in the lake.

Worthy are the Irish to dwell in this their land,
A race of men renowned in war, in peace, in faith.[3]

CHAPTER V

The Vikings

S UDDEN AND TERRIFYING, the fury of the Northmen
struck the monasteries at this moment when art, literature,
and learning had reached their full flower under the patronage
of the Church. In the year 795 Vikings raided the island of
Lambay off the east coast near Dublin, and from then on there
was no respite. Soon the country was the victim of pirate
attacks on all sides and these first raids were but the preliminary
to three hundred turbulent years of struggle. The wars of the
Gaedhil with the Gaill are well recorded by the historical
writers, and in view of the long span of freedom from outside
aggression which Ireland had enjoyed it is hardly surprising
to find these invasions from the north make such an impression
on the annalists.

Ireland, of course, was not the only victim of the Northmen.
At this time a number of causes had combined to produce the
great freebooting expeditions from the Scandinavian lands.
Landless younger sons, unsuccessful pretenders to petty
thrones and young men who simply sought adventure sailed in
their long ships to all the coasts and rivers of Europe. There had
been sporadic forays in earlier times—the unknown pirates who
raided Tory Island off the north coast of Ireland in the seventh
century may well have been Norsemen—and there had been
some peaceful colonization as in the Shetlands. But it was at
the end of the eighth century that large-scale Viking expeditions
set sail. So widely and so freely did these Scandinavians range
the western seas that it is frequently difficult to distinguish the
nationalities of the raiders, but the first pirate attackers of the
remote north-west and west—Orkneys, Shetlands, Hebrides,
Man, Scotland, and Ireland—were the Norse, who remained
always the chief aggressors in Ireland.

THE FIRST ONSLAUGHT

The first raids were mainly sudden onslaughts on island and coastal monasteries and in the early years of the ninth century the annalists record the plundering of Inishmurray, Bangor, Downpatrick, and many others, even the seemingly untempting Skellig, by 'these valiant, wrathful, foreign, purely-pagan people'.[1] The fierce and sudden raids inspired urgent terror in the virtually defenceless monasteries, and a quatrain written in Irish in the margin of a ninth-century manuscript records the comfort which the scribe finds in a storm on the sea:

> Fierce and wild is the wind to-night,
> It tosses the tresses of the sea to white;
> On such a night as this I take my ease;
> Fierce Northmen only course the quiet seas.[2]

This very manuscript, the St Gall Priscian, was later carried to Switzerland—perhaps by a monk driven into exile by the same Viking terror.

Until about 830 the attacks were sporadic, but then the Viking Turgesius came with a 'great royal fleet' to the north and 'assumed the sovereignty of all the foreigners of Ireland'. Other fleets followed and the Norse now made determined efforts to found colonies. Turgesius was checked at the mouth of the Erne and the mouth of the Shannon but established a stronghold by the Dubh-Linn (black pool) at the ford of the Liffey. Here he was master of the earliest Viking state recorded in the history of Western Europe and from here and from his other bases on Lough Neagh and Lough Ree he ravaged all parts of Ireland. Birr, Seir Kieran, Castledermot, Clonmac-noise, Lorrha, Terryglass, Inishcaltra, Clonenagh, Emly—one by one the great monasteries were plundered and burned, abbots and monks murdered and sanctuaries defiled. Ota, wife of Turgesius, gave heathen oracles from the Clonmacnoise altar and he himself assumed the abbacy at Armagh. He was finally captured by the king of Meath and was drowned in Lough Owel, but the ravaging went on.

Not only Dublin but other harbour-settlements were founded, such as Waterford at the head of the long fjord-like estuary of Loch dá chaech, and Wexford on the shallow land-locked bay at the south-east corner of the island. These Viking settlements themselves became the prey of new hordes of marauders who appeared with strong fleets shortly after the death of Turgesius, and now in a series of savage sea-fights along the east coast Viking fought Viking, the *Finn-ghaill* (fair foreigners; Norse) fiercely resisting the attacks of the *Dubh-ghaill* (dark foreigners; perhaps Danes) and finally triumphing after first having suffered some bloody defeats. Dublin, under a new Norse leader, Olaf the White, emerged from the carnage as a small but strong and menacing kingdom. In the meantime an Irish high king of courage and enterprise, Aed Finnliaith, of the northern Ui Néill, had succeeded; he destroyed the Norse strongholds in the north of Ireland and followed this by defeating the Norse in a sea-battle on Lough Foyle in A.D. 867; then, in a decisive engagement near Drogheda, his army, carrying the *Bachall Íosa* and an en-shrined relic of the True Cross, routed a mixed force of Norse and Irish. After this, no Viking settlements were re-established north of Dublin and the brunt of the ravaging fell on middle and southern Ireland. A Munster chronicler describes 'im-mense floods and countless sea-vomitings of ships and boats and fleets so that there was not a harbour nor a land-port nor a dún nor a fortress nor a fastness in all Mumha without floods of Danes and pirates', and he goes on, 'so that they made spoil-land and sword-land and conquered land of her, throughout her breadth and generally; and they ravaged her chieftainries and her privileged churches and her sanctuaries; and they rent her shrines and her reliquaries and her books'.[3]

That this account is not altogether rhetorical exaggeration is amply confirmed by the archaeological evidence. The museums of Scandinavia are rich in Irish material of a form that gives direct evidence of the looting. Most of the finds come from Viking graves, some of which date from quite early in the ninth century, and are, in the main, ecclesiastical objects—mountings ripped from shrines and often altered into brooches, the shrines themselves, hanging-bowls and their escutcheons. There are also some secular pieces, scales, weights, drinking-horn mountings, horse-trappings, and bucket-mountings. Many Norse ladies at this time were buried wearing ornaments fashioned from fragments of Irish shrines. It was 'high fashion' according to Shetelig to wear a third, foreign, brooch on the breast between the normal tortoise brooches. But the value attached by the Vikings and their womenfolk to their plundered treasure is even better illustrated by the runic inscription 'Ranvaig owns this casket' added to an early house-shaped shrine found in Norway and now in the National Museum in Copenhagen. The shrine, adorned in a monastic workshop to contain the relics of a saint, had become a Viking lady's jewel box.

If the nationalities of the invaders are not always clear from the accounts in the annals, there is little ambiguity in the material evidence. The vast majority of Irish finds in Scandinavia have come from Norwegian graves and represent pillage carried off in the early raids; the Viking material that accompanies them in the burials provides, in many cases, dating evidence for the Irish finds and strengthens the view that they are of the styles of the eighth and early ninth centuries. The number of such finds which must have reached Norway in a comparatively short space of time is so great that, as Professor Bøe has put it when describing one of them, 'It would have been necessary to reconstruct the Viking expeditions to Ireland on archaeological evidence, even if every literary record were lacking.'[4] A similar picture is given by the Viking finds in Ireland.

Plates 42–45

Figs. 4c, 4e

Fig. 31a

Some few Irish objects are known from the other Scan-dinavian countries but these do not seem to have been brought there as Viking loot. Much of the Irish material in Denmark derives ultimately from Norway. The finds from Sweden include the remarkable crosier-head from Ekerø. This was found on a habitation site which covered many centuries and which included objects from many lands. The well-known bucket-mounting from Birka was found on a similar site.

The Viking material found in Ireland outside the towns is suprisingly meagre and is largely confined to the time of the first raids. Apart from the great cemetery at Islandbridge (from which derives by far the greatest bulk of material) and six other burials, almost all the finds are stray and there are few sites that can be identified as Viking. The Norse, of course, founded the towns of Ireland and many of these towns still retain their Scandinavian names, Wexford, Waterford, Arklow, Wicklow being obvious examples. The name of Dublin is Irish but its neighbourhood still preserves the place-names of the Scandinavian kingdom—Dalkey, Lambay, Skerries, Howth, Leixlip—and the district immediately north of Dublin bears the Irish name Fingal—'the land of the foreigners'. The present English names of three of the provinces, Ulster, Munster, Leinster, contain Irish words combined according to Norwegian rules and the very name Ireland is Norse in origin. Since the Viking settlements became our modern towns, growing and being rebuilt throughout the centuries, few known Viking sites are available for excavation. Though most excavated ring-forts and crannogs of the period have produced some objects of Norse origin, none can be pointed to as a Viking dwelling; this despite the strong tradition still current that the Danes were the builders of the forts, a tradition which owes its origin to Giraldus Cambrensis, who attributed all the earthworks to the Norse under Turgesius. 'For the Irish', he wrote, 'attach no importance to castles, they make the woods their stronghold and the bogs their trenches.'[5]

One extant earthwork may, with some certainty, be identified as a Norse settlement though it still awaits excavation. This is the site at Annagassan, Co. Louth—an irregularly circular area surrounded by a bank and a fosse outside. Annagassan is the Linn Duachaill of the annals, where the Norse established themselves about A.D. 841 and constructed a *longphort* (ship-camp). The earthwork here is in an appropriate position for such a stronghold, for the river flows immediately close by and it is within a very short distance of the sea.

It is to Dublin, however, that we must turn for the main archaeological evidence of the northern colonization. The dwellings and the burial mounds of the foreigners have been levelled in the growth of the capital, but the Thingmote or meeting-place of the Norse was still to be seen in Dublin in the seventeenth century and was referred to as 'the fortified hill near the College'. Hoggen Green, the old name for College Green, referred to the burial mounds (*haugen*) of the Vikings which stood in the neighbourhood. But this is the centre of modern Dublin and it is fortunate that the great cemetery lay outside the city at Islandbridge-Kilmainham where it escaped destruction until the Great Southern Railway was built in the mid-nineteenth century. This was the most considerable Viking cemetery in the colonies and although many of the finds were lost and no record was ever made of their association, the grave-goods that found their way to the National Museum not only instruct us on the weapons of the Dublin Norse—over thirty swords, numerous spearheads, axes, shield umbos and arrow-heads were found—but also tell us something of their more peaceful activities. The burial rite was inhumation, as we learn from some few graves which were scientifically excavated in the 1930's, but evidence for cremation, which was extremely rare in the Norse colonies, is provided by the presence of bent

Fig. 26. Furnishings of a Viking grave at Island-bridge. Lengths: sword 39 in., spear 20⅜ in., axe 6¼ in.

swords. This practice of mutilating swords before burial was in Norway strictly confined to cremation burials. One complete set of grave-goods was found with a skeleton in 1938 and comprised a sword of the usual Norwegian ninth-century type with a straight cross-bar and triangular pommel, a spearhead of Norse-Irish type, an axe and—a great rarity in Ireland—four nails and two iron handles probably from a wooden coffin.

Some of the swords show a high degree of craftsmanship in the ornament of their pommels, with silver strips beaten into grooves in the iron, chequer patterns in silver, and one very fine example richly gilt and decorated with small silver circles set in niello. The most common type among the Irish finds is the distinctively Norwegian sword of the early ninth century, which occurs everywhere along the line of the early Norse raids. More unusual outside Norway is a fine Frankish sword of a type that is rare in Britain and Ireland; its five-lobed pommel has a meandering vegetable pattern in silver and carries on the upper surface of the guard the name Hartolfr—the name of the sword cutler. Another example of this type is known from Ireland: the excellently preserved sword found in a bog at Ballinderry, Co. Westmeath, later discovered to be the site of the crannog Ballinderry 1. In this case there is a vine pattern on the silver-plated guard, with the name Hiltepreht on its upper surface. The name Ulfberht which appears on one side of the blade is indication of manufacture on a grand scale. It occurs once at Islandbridge, frequently in Norway, as well as on Carolingian swords.

Most of the Islandbridge swords are from the ninth century and together with the evidence of the tortoise brooches from the women's graves, which belong to a well-dated series, they confirm that the cemetery was open before A.D. 850. This date agrees perfectly with the annals. Tools and implements are rare in the Norse colonies but knives, hammers, forge-tongs, and sickles come from Islandbridge, as do also spindle-whorls

Plate 47

Plate 46

and linen-smoothers. Four sets of bronze scales and the set of ornamented weights referred to in Chapter IV show the Vikings in their rôle as traders. This aspect of their activity is rather a forgotten one in the Irish annals but is frequently mentioned in the Icelandic sagas—'From London Gunlaug sailed with some traders to Dublin.' The description in *The Wars of the Gaedhil with the Gaill* of the sack of Viking Limerick after the battle of Sulchóid though doubtless exaggerated, suggests something of the wealth of a Viking city.

> They followed them also into the fort and slaughtered them on the streets and in the houses . . . and the fort was sacked by them after that. They carried off their jewels and their best property, and their saddles beautiful and foreign; their gold and their silver; their beautifully woven cloth of all colours and of all kinds; their satins and silken cloth, pleasing and variegated, both scarlet and green, and all sorts of cloth in like manner. They carried away their soft, youthful, bright, matchless girls; their blooming silk-clad young women; and their active, large, and well-formed boys. The fort and the good town they reduced to a cloud of smoke and to red fire afterwards. The whole of the captives were collected on the hills of Saingel. Every one of them that was fit for war was killed, and every one that was fit for a slave was enslaved.[6]

Such luxuries as silk, satin, and chased leather might have been obtained from the east, for we must remember that these cities belonged not so much to Ireland as to the world of the wandering Viking sea-captain who would put in one day to Cadiz, another day at the wharfs of Paris, and would come to Dublin, the great emporium of his people in the West, to exchange his silver for slaves in the markets there. The many Norse loan-words in the Irish language referring to trade (*margadh*, a market; *mangaire*, a merchant, etc.) shed further light on these activities.

The other Viking burials so far known in Ireland have little to add to our knowledge. The grave-find from Larne and most of the find from the Donnybrook mound have been lost and the others were of the usual type: ninth-century style tortoise brooches accompanied by a bronze bowl in the woman's grave at Ballyholme; at Arklow, in another woman's grave, very fine tenth-century brooches and a silver chain; while the man's grave at Clifden contained the usual weapons. The Navan finds present features of greater interest.

In 1845 when a railway cutting was being made at Navan a burial came to light comprising the skeletons of two humans, the skull of a horse, a bronze bridle-bit and harness plate, iron rings plated with bronze and seven ornamented gilt-bronze mountings of eighth-century date in technique and design. All the material is Irish but the presence of the horse skull and grave-goods is foreign to Irish Christian practice and suggests a Norwegian burial. In confirmation of this, identical series of mountings have come from Viking graves in that country. In a woman's grave of the early ninth century at Gausel, the small gilt-bronze plaques with eyes for attachment lay actually on the horse's skull and a third set is known from Soma. The Navan find again belongs to the early period, the time of constant expeditions which gave rise to the saying preserved in one of the Icelandic sagas:

> Fare thou south to Dublin
> That track is most renowned.[7]

THE IRISH REACTION

The ninth-century onslaught, heavily though it fell upon Ireland, was at least directed against a society which was in full vigour, and the reaction against the Norse, when it came, was strong. The determined attack of the mid-century, augmented by constant fresh fleets from Norway, although it succeeded in lodging Viking settlements on the Irish coast, failed in what seems to have been its ultimate aim, to conquer Ireland for the Norse. When the outbreak of a dynastic struggle in Norway deprived the western waters of new fleets from the homeland, the Scandinavian settlements in Ireland, under constant pressure from the Irish, shrank in power and menace, and about the year 880 there began an uneasy lull in the Viking storm.

This powerful challenge had provoked not only a military response from Christian Ireland. A new impetus was given to movements which had begun shortly before the first raids. The raiders had carried off precious metalwork, but they valued illuminated manuscripts not at all and many are the lamentations in the annals for the 'drowning' of books in the lakes and seas of Ireland; but just as the works of Irish goldsmiths found in Norwegian graves illustrate the direct effect of the Norse attack, so another, indirect, effect is illustrated by the many Irish manuscripts now in the libraries of Europe. A new Irish missionary movement to the Continent had begun in the eighth century; when the quiet monasteries of Ireland became the scene of pillage and slaughter this movement increased and the wandering Irish monks were many on the roads of the Carolingian Empire. The situation on the Continent had changed, however, and no longer could great Columban monasteries grow up around the hermits' cells to become centres of religion in pagan or half-Christian lands, as in the seventh century. Now the Church was organized on the Continent on diocesan and territorial lines and into this system the Irish monks, to whom such organization was foreign, fitted with difficulty, if at all. Thus they often came into conflict with continental bishops who found it necessary to legislate for the control of 'wandering Irish bishops', and sometimes accused them of heresy. As early as the middle of the eighth century the great English missionary and organizer St Boniface wrote letters to Pope Zachary, complaining of the Irishman St Virgil of Salzburg, that he had heretically taught the existence of the antipodes—'that there are another world and other men under the earth, and another sun and moon'.[8] Virgil himself had appealed successfully to the Pope in a dispute with Boniface about the Sacrament of Baptism.

The character of the movement of Irish monks to Europe in the early ninth century is therefore different from that of the great missionary movement of the seventh century. Charle-magne and his successors welcomed them to the courts of the empire, firstly it would seem because of their holiness, but also certainly because they brought with them the learning of the Irish schools. Frequently they also carried Irish books with them, no doubt to save them from destruction, and from these books we gain an idea not only of the development of the art of manuscript illumination in Ireland, which has already been described, but also of the state of knowledge and scholarship in western Europe at the time of Charlemagne. For this purpose the writings of the Irishman Dicuil, who was at the Carolin-gian court in the early ninth century, are of some importance. They include tracts on grammar, on astronomy, and on geography. But it was in the second half of the ninth century that Irish scholars reached their greatest renown in Europe. At Liége, Sedulius Scottus and his companions, Fergus, Blandus, Marcus, Dubthach, and Beuchell formed a circle of courtier-scholars whose standard of learning was as high as the Europe of the day could offer. They wrote works on a variety of sub-jects, chiefly grammar, philosophy, and theology, and their writings display acquaintance with many classical authors and show a fair knowledge of Greek. Some of these works were written on the Continent, some were probably written in Ireland, and there are fairly frequent references to Ireland, to

Irishmen, or to Irish affairs. In one of the poems Sedulius him-self celebrates an Irish victory over the Norsemen.

Another group of Irish scholars at the same period was gathered at Laon in the kingdom of Charles the Bald about a much greater man than Sedulius—Johannes Eriugena. Eriugena was a scholar with a good knowledge of Latin and a fair knowledge of Greek; he was famous in his own time for his translation of the Pseudo-Dionysius, but in his philo-sophical writings he went far beyond the thought of his time and in these he was a worthy precursor of the great schoolmen of the thirteenth century. The Neo-Platonism which he taught caused his writings to be judged heretical and as a result he had little influence on the thought of the ninth century, but he was the only scholar in that dark age to produce a complete philo-sophical synthesis, the *De Divisione Naturae*, the first great work of its kind in western Europe.

Besides these scholars and writers there were many more in Carolingian Europe, often making pilgrimages to Bobbio, St Gall, and other places associated with the Irish saints of the seventh century, or following the road to the tomb of St Peter at Rome. Heiric of Auxerre, writing in the ninth century, says: 'Why should I mention Ireland, of which almost the whole people, despising the dangers of the sea, migrate with their crowd of philosophers, to our shores.'[9]

The scattering of monks and scholars was a natural result of the raids from the sea and indeed the description of the plight of Ireland which the rhetoric of the chroniclers supplies would suggest that the religious life of the monasteries and the pro-duction of works of art must have become impossible in the ninth century. A great many craftsmen must have been murdered in the monastic schools and scriptoria, and countless books destroyed. But neither monasticism nor art came to an end. It is true that during the centuries of the Viking wars the fragile art of manuscript illumination died, never to revive again. There was also a decline in the quality of metalworking and a disappearance, temporary in some cases, of the more elaborate techniques of the earlier period—millefiori, filigree and chip-carving are absent, enamels are rare and those used are of inferior quality. Exquisite delicacy and minute intricacy no longer appear in the work of the goldsmiths, and other changes come about which were due to the troubles of the time.

Some changes, however, were due to a renewed increase in contacts between the Irish and the outside world. They appear most clearly in the art of figure-carving in stone, which reached its zenith in these troubled centuries. The art itself, indeed, was not derived, for it had been moribund in Europe for some centuries—the last sculptors in the classical tradition of the Mediterranean had worked in seventh-century Northumbria —but the Irish carvers of the High Crosses drew now upon the stock of Byzantine and Carolingian iconography to depict in sandstone or in granite Scriptural themes which elsewhere appeared in ivories, frescoes, or perhaps stucco.

THE SCRIPTURE CROSSES

Figure-sculpture, and even, in two cases, sculpture illustrative of Scriptural scenes, had appeared on the crosses of the Slievenaman group, already described, but was completely subordinate to the abstract ornament and was usually confined to the base. Outside the very limited area wherein the crosses of this group are found, there are other monuments, distributed over a wide area of the midland plain between the Shannon and the Irish Sea, on which the tentative efforts of the sculptors to adapt the High Cross to the portrayal of figured scenes may be discerned. In these transitional crosses the sculpture is no longer confined to the base, but now appears on the shaft itself, and the sculptor was required to accommodate his narrative art to the tall narrow rectangle thus provided. The final solution to this problem was simple and effective. Each of the main faces of the cross-shaft was divided by mouldings into rectangular panels of a convenient shape, and a different scene or episode was depicted in each panel; but in the meantime several expedients were attempted. In and near the great monastery of Clonmacnoise there were several crosses and shafts in which a continuous, if somewhat crowded, composition fills the main member of the cross from top to bottom. The carvings on these monuments have no Scriptural content but seem to continue the mysterious themes of the Slievenaman carvings, with horsemen, hounds, deer, etc.; some fabulous animals, including a lion-like beast with a foliate tail, like those on the Pictish slabs of Scotland; and, on the north shaft at Clonmacnoise, a squatting cross-legged human figure, much weathered now, on whose head Dr Françoise Henry has discerned the antlers of a stag, of which she has justly remarked: 'One thinks of Cernunnos, the Deer-god of the Gaulish Pantheon.'[10] Two shafts at Clonmacnoise itself, a shaft from Banagher, some miles from the monastery to the south, and a cross at Bealin, some miles away to the north, are of this type, but the south cross at Clonmacnoise is a compromise of a different sort. This retains the short shaft and stocky proportions of the Slievenaman monuments (although with a smaller ring) and has also the panels of abstract ornament, including spirals, and the massive bosses, but into the midst of this ornament a figured panel has been introduced, depicting the Crucifixion, with a long-robed Christ and attendant figures in a composition closely resembling that of the Athlone plaque.

Plate 54
Fig. 28g

At the Columban monastery of Kells, to which the monks of Iona had come early in the ninth century, there stands a fine cross of this transitional type, and there are others in the east

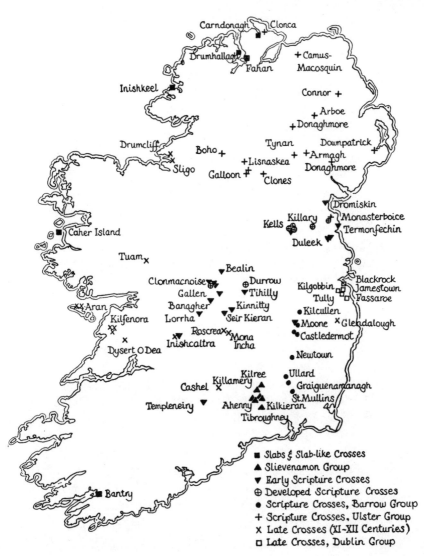

Carndonagh + Clonca
Drumhallagh
Fahan
Inishkeel
+ Camus-
Macosquin
Connor +
+ Arboe
+ Donaghmore
Drumcliff
Boho +
Tynan
Lisnaskea
Galloon +
+ Clones
Downpatrick
+ Armagh
Donaghmore
Sligo
Dromiskin
Killary
Monasterboice
Kells
Termonfechin
Duleek
Caher Island
Tuam
Bealin
Clonmacnoise
Durrow
Gallen
Tihilly
Banagher
Kinnitty
Lorrha
Seir Kieran
Aran
Roscrea
Mona
Kilfenora
Inishcaltra
Incha
Dysert O Dea
Blackrock
Kilgobbin
Jamestown
Tully
Fassaroe
Kilcullen
Moone
Glendalough
Castledermot
Newtown
Kilree
Ullard
Cashel
Killamery
Graiguenamanagh
St Mullins
Templeneiry
Ahenny
Kilkieran
Tibroughney
Bantry

■ Slabs & Slab-like Crosses
▲ Slievenamon Group
▼ Early Scripture Crosses
⊕ Developed Scripture Crosses
● Scripture Crosses, Barrow Group
+ Scripture Crosses, Ulster Group
X Late Crosses (XI-XII Centuries)
□ Late Crosses, Dublin Group

Fig. 27. Map showing distribution of figure-carved High Crosses.

Plate 55

midlands at Duleek and Termonfechin. The cross of Patrick and Columba at Kells (it is so called from an Irish inscription it bears) is in proportions like the south cross at Clonmacnoise and it also has a shaft undivided by panelling. However, a number of scenes are here represented, including Daniel in the Den of Lions, the Three Children in the fiery furnace, Adam and Eve, and Cain and Abel, but the scenes do not fully cover any face of the shaft, which still has large areas of decorative carving, including the inhabited vine-scroll. On the crosses of Duleek and Termonfechin the arrangement is similar.

A part from the appearance of figure-carving on the shafts, the transitional crosses differ from those of the Slievenaman group in that interlacing and animal-ornament now play a much greater part in the decoration, replacing the watch-spring spirals of the southern crosses. Both at Clonmacnoise and at Kells the full process of the transition can be observed, since both sites have fully developed Scripture crosses, the west cross at Clonmacnoise, indeed, being commonly known as 'The Cross of the Scriptures'. And the approximate limiting dates of the process are supplied by two of the crosses in the Clon-macnoise area. That of Bealin has an inscription to the effect that it was erected by one Tuathgal. There was an abbot of this name (then a common one in Ireland) at Clonmacnoise, who died in 811, and on this, unhappily not wholly satisfactory, evidence the cross has been dated. The ornament, however, which includes the Lindisfarne bird, supports the inference from the inscription. The Cross of the Scriptures bears an inscription, now incomplete, but read by Petrie more than a century ago. His drawing of the letters which still remain is quite accurate, so that his reading may be accepted. The inscription requested a prayer for Flann, king of Munster, who died in 904.

The High Crosses of Ireland, of the developed Scriptural type of the tenth century, are architectural in proportion and composition, with an orderly and systematic iconographic sculptural scheme that is, essentially, a premature manifestation of Romanesque art. Strangely, these themes from the Scriptures which the Irish sculptors learned to carve on the High Crosses never adorned churches in Ireland, for fashions had changed and the portrayal of narrative scenes had been abandoned when doorways and chancel arches came to be embellished with carving in the twelfth century.

Fig. 28. Scenes from Scripture Crosses. a. Noah's Ark (Killary, w. cross); b. Adam and Eve and Cain and Abel (Monasterboice, Muiredach's Cross); c. Sacrifice of Isaac (Durrow); d. David playing the harp (Castledermot, s. cross); e. Baptism of Christ (Kells, broken cross); f. Soldiers guarding the tomb of Christ (Clonmacnoise, Cross of the Scriptures); g. Hunting scene (Bealin).

The finest monuments of this art are the Cross of Muiredach and the west cross at Monasterboice, the market cross and the broken cross at Kells, the cross of Durrow, and the Cross of the Scriptures at Clonmacnoise. The arrangement of the carving is similar on all, with some variations, and the Cross of Muiredach may stand as the type for the rest.

This like the others is of sandstone, the shaft and head being carved from the one block, but unlike most of them it bears an inscription, asking for a prayer for Muiredach. There were two abbots of this name at Monasterboice, one of whom died in the eighth century and the other, to whom the monument is generally attributed, in 923. The cross, including the base, is 17 feet 8 inches high and of massive proportions, carved on the two main faces (those looking east and west) with figured panels and on the narrower sides of the shaft with panels of ornament. On the crossing and arms of each face an elaborate composition has been attempted. That on the east face depicts

Plates 56, 57

the Crucifixion, with two angels over the shoulders of Christ (who is shown nude and with bound ankles, as is usual in carvings of this group), the lance- and sponge-bearers, and other attendant figures; that on the west face depicts the Last Judgment, where Christ is shown in the so-called 'Osiris attitude' with crossed flowering sceptre and cross, and the damned are arranged on one hand, the blessed on the other, while in the centre below the feet of Christ, Michael weighs the souls of the dead and Satan attempts to upset the balance. The smaller panels on the shaft are arranged so that scenes from the New Testament occur below the Crucifixion and scenes from the Old Testament below the Judgment. The carving of the episodes is in bold and rounded relief and the sculptor, while preserving a perfectly orderly arrangement of the figures, has succeeded in imparting to them a lively variety of expression and gesture. The figures themselves are of considerable interest because of the details of costume and personal ornament to be seen; the fiercely moustached soldiers in baggy breeches, carrying Viking swords; the tonsured ecclesiastics in long hooded robes, holding books or crosiers. On the narrow sides of the cross-shaft are decorative panels of animal-interlace, bosses and scrolls, fret-patterns, and the Northumbrian inhabited vine-scroll. One of the most interesting features of the cross is its apex, which is a carving of a gabled building with a roof of shingles or tiles. Muiredach's cross must be placed last in the series of developed Scripture crosses of the south midlands and it marks the high point of the style. At about the time of its erection a new Viking onslaught began on Ireland, falling most heavily on the southern half of the country, and the later development of the Scripture crosses took place north of the central plain. These monuments show a considerable lengthen-ing of the shaft, to accommodate more figured panels, and a gradual diminution of the ring. One of the first, and perhaps the finest of them, is at Monasterboice itself—the great west cross, which is the tallest in the country—and the others are distributed across the mid-Ulster lowlands from the Erne to Lough Neagh and Belfast Lough, at Donaghmore, Co. Tyrone, Camus Macosquin, Co. Derry, Arboe, Co. Tyrone, Armagh, Clones, Co. Monaghan, Boho, Co. Fermanagh, and Drumcliff, Co. Sligo. There is a slow decline in the quality of the carving, and some curious and clumsy features appear, such as a slightly projecting collar of ornament below the ring. Finally the whole scheme of figured panels is aban-doned and in the last examples, as at Boho and Drumcliff, which are probably of the early eleventh century, abstract ornament has again invaded the main faces of the shaft.

Fig. 27

Parallel to the series of Scripture crosses of the midland plain there is a small regional group that has a similar iconographic arrangement but a very distinctive character. The crosses of this group are situated in the valley of the river Barrow, at Castledermot, Moone, Kilcullen, Graigenamanagh, St Mullins, and Ullard in south-east Ireland, and they are carved not in sandstone but in granite, the local stone. The intractable nature of this medium has influenced the style of the carving, which is rendered in a low relief of two planes. The figures, almost diagrammatic in their simplicity, have all the quaint-ness and charm of primitive or rustic art, and this is most apparent on the finest monument of the series, the slenderly proportioned High Cross, standing on a high plinth at the

Columban monastery of Moone, Co. Kildare. The Scriptural scenes depicted include the Crucifixion, the Flight into Egypt, the meeting of Paul and Antony in the desert, Daniel in the Den of Lions, the Miracle of the Loaves and Fishes, and the Twelve Apostles ('standing like dolls in a village shop'—Dr Henry), while fabulous animals and snakes fill other panels.

These fabulous creatures relate the Barrow crosses both to the Slievenaman group and to the transitional crosses of the Midlands. Most of the Barrow monuments also carry panels of fat loosely coiled spirals, looking rather like toothpaste squeezed from a tube and quite unlike the precise and fine spiral ornament of the Slievenaman group. The system of linked spirals employed is an exact repetition of that used by Mycenaean goldsmiths more than two thousand years before; here it, together with the fabulous animals, strongly suggests the influence of Pictish Scotland. In most cases the spiral panels reinforce the impression of a child-like art conveyed by the figured scenes—the sculptor, having failed to set out his work properly before beginning to carve, frequently finds that he must squeeze the last part of his composition into an inadequate space in a corner of the panel.

It has been suggested that the idea of the Scripture cross was developed in the Barrow valley and its region, under the influence of the ecclesiastical reform spirit of the *Céli Dé*, who were most numerous in this part of the country, and that the granite crosses are mainly of ninth-century date, antedating the sandstone monuments of the midlands. Dr Henry points out that together with a revival of asceticism the anchorites introduced new intellectual preoccupations, 'subtilizing on the notion of sin, on permitted and forbidden things, on ascetic methods . . . working on the hidden meaning of liturgy'.[11] Most of the Scripture crosses are not associated with monas-teries which were centres of the *Céli Dé* movement and there is no clear connexion between the ideas of the *Céli Dé* and the iconography of the crosses; nonetheless there is probably some truth in Dr Henry's view. A general revival of intellectual interest in religion and of religious devotion took place towards the end of the ninth century, probably largely as a result of the impulse given by the *Céli Dé*. This revival manifested itself in a number of ways. There was a fresh movement to the Continent at the beginning of the tenth century, not, this time, of philosophers and of scholars, but of simple missionaries; there was a religious and devotional tendency in verse; there was a growth of interest in Scriptural themes. A long poem of the late tenth century, *Saltair na Rann*, a verse history of the Old Testament and the Life of Christ, provides a literary parallel to the Scripture crosses. This general elaboration of religious themes seems, however, to be a feature rather of the tenth century, when the purely ecclesiastical and liturgical movement of the *Céli Dé* was already in decline. The figured scenes of the Barrow crosses, like most rustic art, are a simplified version of work in a more sophisticated style. They lack inscriptions and, while they are clearly related to the much more accomplished work of the Slievenaman and Midland groups, they contain in themselves no safe guide to precise dating. It seems reasonable, however, to regard them as humbler renderings of the transitional and Scripture crosses of the midlands and to infer that they were erected mainly in the tenth century.

THE ROUND TOWERS

It was at this time also that the stone-masons added to the Irish landscape what is still one of its most striking features; the tall, gracefully tapering, conical-capped Round Towers. There are still about eighty of these surviving in whole or in part on the sites of the early monasteries. A delightful Irish version of the

Plates 10, 12, 63

early *campanili* of Italy, they functioned more like the Muslim minarets; from the windows of the topmost storey a monk rang his handbell to the four cardinal points; the slender shape rising above the trees guided the pilgrim on his way to visit the foundation and shrine of some holy saint; the tall *cloicthech* (literally 'bell-house') gave unity and form to the cluster of huts and little churches and gave also a feeling of security, even if it was often illusory, to the community.

The towers were first built probably in the early tenth century, primarily, as is clear from their name, as belfries, but also, from an early stage in their development, to serve as places of safety and refuge for both monks and valuables, as some details of their structure reveal. In almost all, the doorway is some ten or fifteen feet above the ground and can be reached only by ladder. Access from floor to floor within the tower was also by removable ladder, and only one narrow window supplied light to each storey, the windows being so arranged that each commands a different aspect. The floors themselves were usually of wood (although three towers have stone floors) but the conical roof was of corbelled stone construction. The Round Towers were all solidly built of mortared stone, but on very shallow foundations so that, apart from the destruction caused by war or lightning, many of them have collapsed and others, such as the tower at Kilmacduagh, which is one of the tallest, have listed perilously from the perpendicular. Perhaps to overcome this weakness, a few of the towers were built on square, octagonal, or circular plinths. The masonry itself shows a steady progression in finish, from the rough unworked stones and spall-packed mortar joints of early examples such as that at Castledermot, to the fine ashlar work, often with elaborate joggled joints, of the twelfth century, as in the tower at Drumlane or O'Rourke's tower at Clonmacnoise. The finest of the whole series, the Round Tower at Ardmore, Co. Waterford, is one of the latest, dating from about the close of the twelfth century. It is tall and elegantly proportioned, with external string courses marking the levels of the floors, and with a simple adornment of Romanesque mouldings and carvings. Like the other late towers, that at Ardmore is built of ashlar blocks carefully cut not only to the curve of the wall but also to supply an entasis. In general, however, the early simplicity of form was retained and only two of the Round Towers (at Kildare and Timahoe) have elaborately carved doorways.

In size alone these buildings are an impressive achievement for a people which had previously attempted no ambitious architecture in stone. They vary in height from about seventy to about a hundred and twenty feet, the taller examples being generally of later date. In design they display a classic simplicity and grace unexpected in the milieu of late Celtic art, with its love of elaborate surface ornament. Yet, although the idea of the towers was almost certainly suggested by foreign belfries, the form was clearly developed in Ireland. It is found in every part of the country and nowhere else except in Scotland, where there are a few Round Towers of the latest period of construction. A few of the small early Irish stone churches—St Kevin's and Trinity at Glendalough, and the little church on Lambay Island—have or had small towers of the same form, which were attached to the church at one end of the roof ridge. These are probably of the early period when the belfries were first being built, but this experiment was soon abandoned and the common practice became the building of the great free-standing tower with its doorway facing the doorway of the small church which it overshadowed, protected, and announced with the note of the

> Sweet little bell
> That is rung on a windy night.[12]

Plates 58–60

Plates 59, 60

Plate 62

Fig. 29

While these new arts in stone were developing in the time of the Viking invasions and wars, the art of illuminating manu-scripts died and that of metalworking suffered a temporary decline. Some new types of metalwork of undoubted Scandi-navian inspiration appear in the tenth century. Native metal-working continued, mainly on a minor scale, but at times capable of producing fairly ambitious objects such as the Kells Crosier, now in the British Museum. This shrine, like so many other Irish reliquaries, has undergone damage and repair at various times and now exhibits work of several periods. It consists of a yew staff encased in bronze, with an ornamental crook-casing and crest of silver, four ornamental bronze knops, and two binding-strips of bronze. The three lower shaft-knops, which were made in the tenth century, give a good idea of the native style in metalworking at this time. Each knop is divided by raised bronze borders into panels, originally silver-coated, containing each a different design of one or two fantastic animals or of rather degenerate interlacing. This division into panels, contrasting with the over-all ornament of the earlier art may be in part derived from the Trewhiddle style of southern England. The tendency is noticeable on some of the late brooches, such as the Killamery brooch (on the back), and is also a feature of the tenth-century crosses which have just been described. The designs are cast in low relief, un-adorned by hatching or filigree, and the ornament depends for its effect on the firm and skilful arrangement of the animal portraits and on their lively and cheerful personality rather than on any delicacy of embellishment. Coating with silver, as on this crosier, or with gold, as on the related Crosier of St Mel, is the sole adornment of the casting. There is a considerable repertoire of animal designs, all in the tradition of native Irish art and closely dependent on what has gone before. Some of

the interlaced designs are badly drawn and degenerate; this
tendency is more pronounced on slightly later works such as
the crosiers of St Dympna and St Mel. Towards the end of the
century the native style, as illustrated by such pieces as the
Clogán Óir bell-shrine, was very debased and the animal-
forms are barely recognizable. The same decline is in evidence

Plates 61, 62

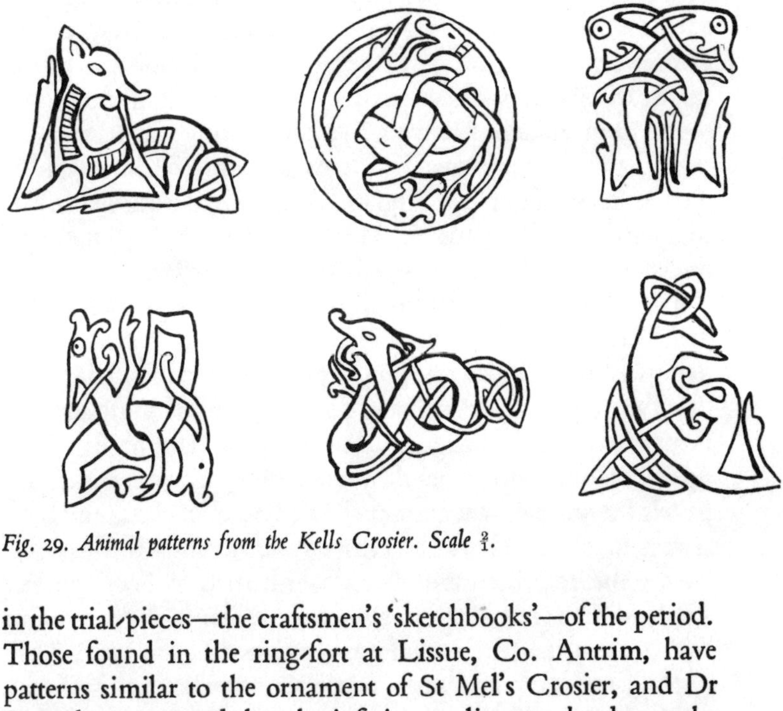

Fig. 29. Animal patterns from the Kells Crosier. Scale ¾.

in the trial-pieces—the craftsmen's 'sketchbooks'—of the period.
Those found in the ring-fort at Lissue, Co. Antrim, have
patterns similar to the ornament of St Mel's Crosier, and Dr
Bersu has suggested that the inferior quality may be due to the
casting of patterns from standard moulds in order to increase
production for markets opened by the Vikings. The theft and
destruction of many sacred objects must certainly have led to
greatly increased demand and thus opened the way to mass-
production and lack of individual finish. By the end of the

century the decline is strikingly apparent and a very strong impulse was required to give new life to the worn-out themes of native metalworking. Such an impulse was, in fact, to appear, contributed partly by the influence of art-forms of the Scandinavians themselves.

Besides works in the pure native style, there are metal objects, principally brooches, of the tenth century which display the strong influence that Scandinavian art had already begun to exert on Ireland. The Hiberno-Viking brooches are generally of silver, without gilding, and this in itself is probably due to the Scandinavians whose traders were at this time dealing in silver from eastern Europe. Typical Viking silver bracelets with their stamped oriental patterns are common in Ireland as well as in Scotland and England. It is indeed possible that, as suggested by Professor Ó Ríordáin, the Vikings not only traded in silver but also exploited the Irish silver mines. The penannular form of the Hiberno-Viking brooches is Irish but their decoration is of Viking inspiration. All of them have free terminals, so that they are a more practical dress-fastening than the Tara type. The dominant decorative motif is an arrange-ment, in the sub-triangular terminals, of four or five large bosses, connected by bands which thus provide and frame panels for animal interlacement. The bodies of the animals are always hatched and are often disconnected. Since the brooches have sometimes been found in dated hoards in Scotland and England they are known to have been in use in the early tenth century; but the type must have developed in the second half of the ninth century, when excellent brooches in the native tradition were still being made, and have taken their form from these Irish brooches while being influenced in the layout of the ornament perhaps by the tortoise brooches.

The thistle brooches of the period have a similar mixed ancestry. These, often very massive silver objects, have, instead of the flattened terminals of the Irish penannular brooches,

Plate 48

Plate 50

spherical terminals with a brambled surface. The head of the pin is also a sphere, often with a flattened top carrying a geometrical pattern, and sometimes the terminal knobs were similarly treated. Thistle brooches are found also in Scandinavia, which is their probable place of origin, but there the flattened surfaces frequently carry, instead of the simple labyrinthine patterns of the Irish examples, animal-ornament in the Jellinge style, as do several of the magnificent examples from the great hoard from Skaill in the Orkneys.

THE STRUGGLE RENEWED

The mixed style of these silver objects is a clear indication of the way in which by the beginning of the tenth century the culture and customs of the Scandinavians were beginning to affect those of the Irish. At first, when the Norse appeared solely as raiders from the sea and were quite external to Irish society, they were regarded with horror in Ireland, more for their heathenism than for their piracy. When Cinnaedh son of Conall, king of the northern Bregia, allied himself with the Norse of Dublin against the Ui Néill of Meath in 850, his action was considered a shocking betrayal of his Christian faith; when he was captured by Maelsechnaill, king of Meath, he was, with general approval, condemned to death by the king and his brehons, and was executed in a manner which expressed the contempt that was felt for his deed; he was 'drowned in a dirty streamlet'. Soon, however, alliances between the Irish and the Norse became commonplace and the foreigners were freely used as pawns in the age-old dynastic and inter-dynastic squabbles of the Irish. Irish methods of warfare changed under Scandinavian influence; that survival of the heroic age, the settling of battles by single combat between the opposing chiefs on the battlefield, now disappeared, and the use of cavalry on land and of fleets on water became for the first time prominent features of Irish warfare. Almost all the words in Irish dealing with ships or parts of ships are derived from the Norse. Manners among the cattle-raiding and pillag-ing aristocratic classes in Ireland can never have been very gentle; now they were further brutalized in the savage fighting of these times and such new barbarous customs as the mutilat-ing and blinding of enemies were practised. From the middle of the ninth century on, cut-throat bands of *Gall-Ghaedhil* (of mixed Norse and Irish blood) infested parts of the country, acting as mercenaries in the incessant warfare of the time.

It was probably, however, the establishment by the Norse of fortified cities and sea-ports, engaged in an extensive foreign trade, that did most to bring about lasting changes in the ancient pastoral economy and the simple political system of Ireland. The relative lull in the Norse attacks from about A.D. 880 to 914 was due to Viking preoccupations overseas, in the homeland and in Northumbria, where the rulers of Dublin had dynastic interests in the kingdom of York. As more and more of Europe became closed to their incursions the Vikings returned in force to Ireland with great fleets deter-mined on conquest, to inaugurate another century of bitter warfare. In this struggle the old Irish political order broke up for ever. The Eoghanacht dynasty, which had ruled Munster since before the time of St Patrick, had already suffered a mortal wound to its power when Cormac mac Cuillenáin, king-bishop of Cashel, and many of the Eoghanacht chiefs were killed in a disastrous defeat of a Munster army by the allied warriors of Leinster and the High King at Belach Mugna in Leinster in 908. The decline of the Ui Néill line itself, the line of the High Kings, began when the High King Niall Glúndubh, leading a great hosting against the Norse of Dublin in 919, was defeated and killed at Islandbridge. In the first half of the tenth century the Vikings showed more than once that they could defeat the strongest forces that Irish chiefs were able to bring against them, even on the rare occasions when inter-dynastic feuds were sufficiently in abeyance for alliances representative of most of Ireland to take the field. But the Norse never profited from these victories by any serious attempt to subdue the whole of Ireland to their rule. They still remained people of the sea, still with no permanent tenure on Irish soil, still regarding their towns of Limerick, Waterford, and Dublin rather as convenient harbours and trading-ports than as bases for conquest. The redoubtable tenth-century kings of Dublin, Sigtryg Gale, Godfred, and Olaf Cuaran were distracted from affairs in Ireland by their efforts to maintain control of York, and their successes against the Irish resulted merely in anarchy.

The situation was one which offered a challenge to able and ambitious men and such a one was the High King Muircher-tach of the northern Ui Néill, who succeeded, in a strenuous campaign in 941, in exacting submission from all the pro-vincial kings and from the Norse cities as well. But he died before he could restore order and stability to the country.

It was from an unlikely quarter that the response to the challenge came—from the hills of eastern County Clare where a minor sept, the Dál Cais, under two able leaders, the brothers Mathghamhain and Brian, engaged about the middle of the century in a long and strenuous guerrilla war against the Norse of Limerick. Mathghamhain seized the kingship of Munster from the Eoghanachta in 963, and he and his brother continued to harass the Vikings until Ivar, the king of Limerick, brought his full power against them in a decisive battle at Sulchóid, in Co. Tipperary, in 967. The two brothers routed the Norse and sacked their rich city.

Mathghamhain was murdered some years later and Brian became king of Munster. For three decades after that, by force, by guile, by initiative and ability, he strengthened his position and built up his power until he succeeded, in 1002, in usurping the high-kingship itself, receiving the submission of the Uí Néill king. Brian Boru was remarkable in the Ireland of his time because he seems to have thought in terms of the feudal organization which had already developed in Europe rather than in terms of the primitive and unstable kingship-system of Ireland. He must have seen his own career as an image of that of Charlemagne, whose life and exploits were a 'mirror for princes' in the later centuries of Dark Age Europe, and when he visited the ecclesiastical capital of Ireland in 1004 he had his scribe enter in the Book of Armagh 'Brian, *Imperator Scottorum*'. Brian in winning his way to power had on occasion availed himself of alliances with Norsemen, but the basis of his whole career was opposition to the foreigners and his life ended in 1014 on the field of the battle in which, as High King of Ireland, he faced a last rally of the Vikings, of Dublin, of Man and the Isles, and of Scandinavia itself, together with their Irish allies, outside the walls of Dublin. This was the battle of Clontarf, celebrated in Scandinavian and Irish literature for the breaking of the power of the Vikings in Ireland.

Chapter VI

Renaissance and Reform

THE BATTLE OF CLONTARF did not bring peace and order to Ireland. On the contrary, it introduced a century and a half of internal disorder. In the time of the Viking wars both the kingship of Cashel and the high-kingship had been usurped by the minor sept of the Dál Cais, most of whose leaders were killed at Clontarf. From then until the Anglo-Norman invasion, the most powerful families of the country were engaged in a futile struggle for the high-kingship and in all that time no one man ever succeeded in having his sovereignty generally accepted, although almost every summer provincial kings were marching into the territory of their neighbours, seeking not only cattle but the kind of power that Brian Boru had commanded. Nevertheless, this was warfare on the scale and of the nature of the immemorial cattle-raids and it did not disrupt the life of the country quite as badly as the Viking attacks had done. The concept of kingship was slowly changing as the Irish became more aware of the feudal structure of Europe; after Brian Boru had set the example, some of the kings seem to have thought of themselves less as the heads of family or tribal groups than as the rulers of states, wielding a royal privilege and patronage, who could display their munificence and increase their dignity by commissioning works of art for the monasteries and churches.

THE NORSE AFTER CLONTARF

The Norse remained important in Irish affairs. They continued to live as separate and distinct communities in their sea-port

Fig. 30. Two early eleventh-century silver pennies minted in Dublin (obverse and reverse). Full size.

towns and to trade overseas in their own fleets. The very existence of their towns must have exercised a gradual influence on the over-simple Irish economy, but for want of excavated sites the social life and material culture of the eleventh and twelfth centuries are much more obscure than those of earlier periods. It is difficult to distinguish the archaeological traces of the Norse themselves for several reasons. They were by now for the most part Christian and no longer buried grave-goods with their dead; the remains of their settlements lie deep under modern Irish cities and are not accessible; furthermore, objects of Norse type, especially weapons, found on Irish sites such as Carraig Aille, and objects of Irish type, as the many ring-pins from Christchurch in Dublin, found on Norse sites, show that by mutual borrowing of equipment the distinction between the two peoples in their material remains was by now largely lost. At Clontarf both Norse and Irish probably fought with the same types of weapons.

At about the beginning of the eleventh century, however, the first coins to be minted in Ireland were struck by Norse moneyers in the city of Dublin. They were issued by the authority of Sitric Silkenbeard (Sitric III), king of Dublin, and were directly copied from silver pennies of Aethelred III who reigned in England from 979 to 1016. Some bear the inscription *Sitric Rex Dyflin* on the obverse and the moneyer's name on the reverse; others were so slavishly copied that besides the word *Dyflin* they have the name of King Aethelred. Coins continued to be minted until about 1150, but the later issues were very degraded and their inscriptions are unintelligible. Runic inscriptions, which are common on the Isle of Man, closely connected with Norse Dublin, are rare in Ireland, only five being known: one from the Great Blasket island off the south-west coast; one from the monastic settlement of Nendrum in the north-east; one on the shaft of a stone cross at Killaloe, Co. Clare, which also has an unintelligible *ogam*;

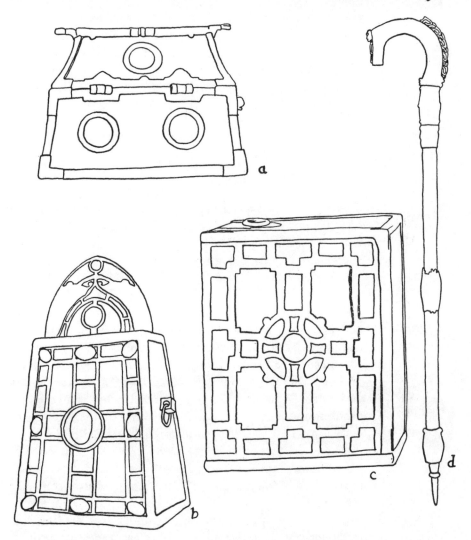

Fig. 31. *Types of shrine. a. House-shaped shrine, Copenhagen; b. St Patrick's bell-shrine; c. St Molaise's book-shrine; d. Crosier of the Abbots, Clonmacnoise staff-shrine. Different scales.*

one, with a small Greek cross, on a stone slab from Beginish island, in Valentia Harbour, Co. Kerry, and one on a small strip of silvered bronze, part of the ornament of a sword, from Greenmount, Co. Louth. These are all of eleventh- and twelfth-century date and in a number of details they show the fusion of Norse and Irish traditions.

METALWORK

Apart from these few meagre remains and the testimony of documentary records, the continued importance of the Norse is attested indirectly by the character of Irish art of the eleventh and twelfth centuries. The tenth-century Irish resurgence under Brian Boru was followed by a cultural revival as the century drew to a close. Brian himself built a number of churches, in the old unadorned style, along the Shannon, that river which had previously been a main highway for Viking marauders; but it was at about the same time, if one is to judge by the evidence of the bronze casings of the bells of St Conall and St Mura, that the quality of ornamental metalworking was at its lowest. Soon after the turn of the century, however, the bronzesmiths began to regain something of the old mastery of their material, and the first phase of the revival of the craft is illustrated by three small book-shrines, two of them dated by inscriptions, made in the half-century after Clontarf: the shrines of the *Soiscél Molaise* (1001–25), the Stowe Missal (1023–52), and the *Breac Maodhóg* (probably about 1050). The bronze-relief ornament of the shrines draws on the old motifs of Irish metalwork to some extent, but displays a development, in which one might see the beginnings of a true Romanesque art, away from the old non-representational themes. The earliest of the three, the *Soiscél Molaise*, has ornament consisting chiefly

Fig. 32. Ringerike pattern from the Kells Crosier.

of little animal-interlace panels which bear some resemblance
to the decoration of the Drumcliff and other early eleventh-
century crosses, but unusual prominence is given to a cast relief
figure of an ecclesiastic surrounded by intertwined animals. In
the Stowe Missal shrine the animal-interlace panels are replaced
by little narrative scenes, such as hounds pulling down a stag,
and, finally, the *Breac Maodhóg* shrine has a splendidly conceived array of human figures, male and female, in bold relief.

Plate 64

Plate 66

But this development, which might have led to an Irish
Romanesque style that would preserve all the native character,
was arrested by a reversion to the old themes of barbarian art,
now under the strong Scandinavian influence. The later
metalwork, like that of the eighth century, is mainly cast
bronze, and some of the earlier techniques, such as enamelling
and filigree-working (but not millefiori) were revived, while new
techniques of silver and niello inlaying were borrowed from the
Scandinavians. The later craftsmen no longer exercised patience
and ingenuity on the production of minute intricacy of pattern.

Their work is on a larger scale, coarser and bolder than that of the eighth century. It is no longer the sheer craftsmanship that is a marvel; the objects rely for their effect rather on skill and ingenuity in design, but at the best period of the late metalwork, at the beginning of the twelfth century, the effect so achieved could be very impressive indeed.

The first centre of metalworking in the new Scandinavian-influenced styles seems to have been the Columban monastery of Kells, Co. Meath. The craftsman who made the collar-

Plate 58   knop of the Kells Crosier, about the middle of the eleventh century, handled with great competence a pattern quite alien to the Irish tradition: a highly stylized acanthus scroll based on a double 'shell-spiral' and executed in an elaborate silver-and-

Fig. 32   niello technique, with fine wavy lines of silver showing against black bands of niello inlay. The design is in pure Ringerike,

Fig. 33   a Scandinavian style of the early eleventh century characterized by loose and sometimes ragged foliate scrolls and interlacings with acanthus motifs, and the technique was one used by Scandinavian metalworkers. The foliate character of Ringerike ornament seems not to have pleased the Irish artists, or their clients, and they soon zoomorphized it. Two book-shrines, of the *Cathach* and the *Misach* of St Columcille, made at about the end of the third quarter of the eleventh century (also, there is reason to believe, at Kells), have interlace patterns in relief, with the loose composition and free ends of Ringerike orna-ment; there are acanthus terminals to some of the tendrils, but also animal heads.

In fact the Ringerike style in its pure forms was as transient as the figured style which had preceded it. The Irish found much more to their taste in the later Scandinavian Urnes style (named from an elaborately carved wooden church in Norway), which was ultimately based on the animal ornament of Irish objects carried off by the Vikings in the eighth century. The constant theme of the Urnes style is a combat between a great

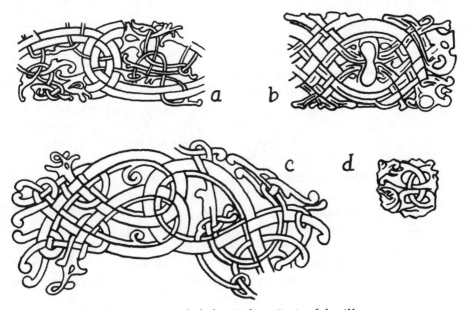

Fig. 33. Irish Ringerike patterns. a. Cathach; b. Misach; c. Crosier of the Abbots, developed; d. Killeshin stone fragment. Not to scale.

ribbon-bodied quadruped and a serpent or serpents who entwine his limbs in their coils. This style was to be given its finest expression in Ireland, since it was readily adapted to the familiar animal-interlace patterns, but its first effect on Irish art was to influence minor details of the zoomorphized Ringerike patterns.

One of the handsomest of all the crosier-shrines, the 'Crosier of the Abbots of Clonmacnoise', is closely related stylistically to the *Cathach* and *Misach* shrines. Here, on the crook, is the same basic pattern of broad double-loop bands, linked at the centre but with free ends at the terminals, caught in a loose mesh of narrower strands. The ornament has been most skilfully adapted to the curves of the crook and is inlaid in

Plate 67

167

silver and niello in the bronze. In it the acanthus has almost disappeared. The animal heads are still there but are somewhat different from those of the book-shrines; they are, in fact, identical with those in the wood-carving of Urnes church, even to the most un-Irish detail that in the pointed ovoid eyes the point is to the front. The junction of crook and shaft, at front and back, is adorned with fierce animal heads, cast in the round with wildly flowing foliate intertwined lappets and whiskers. On the upper and lower knops are triangular panels with geometric or foliate patterns shown in reserve bronze against a background of red and green champlevé enamel. This crosier-shrine, made towards the end of the eleventh century, with its hints of Urnes influence, marks the full maturity of the revived art of metalworking.

The supreme achievements of this art were produced in the first quarter of the twelfth century. There is a whole series of late crosiers, and there are several large metalwork shrines of other sorts. The richly ornamented Innisfallen crosier employs a great variety of ornament, still predominantly Ringerike in character, but the most elaborate of the crosiers is from the monastery of Lismore. This is a heavy object of riveted bronze plates. Like the others of its time it has an openwork bronze crest with large terminal ornaments cast in the round in the form of animal heads with loosely intertwined lobed lappets and moustaches—a relic of the Ringerike style. Ornament is confined to the crest, knops, and binding strip, the main shaft of the crosier being smooth bronze. Each of the barrel-shaped knops has a sort of lattice-work of bronze strips, with large circular settings for enamels at the crossings. In the interstices of the lattice-work are sub-rectangular panels, with wiry patterns in gilt-bronze. These include panels of human inter-lace not unlike those on the crosses of Ahenny and Monaster-boice, and panels of animal interlace which are an early variant of the Irish Urnes style. The enamels of the studs are in

Figs. 34a, 34b

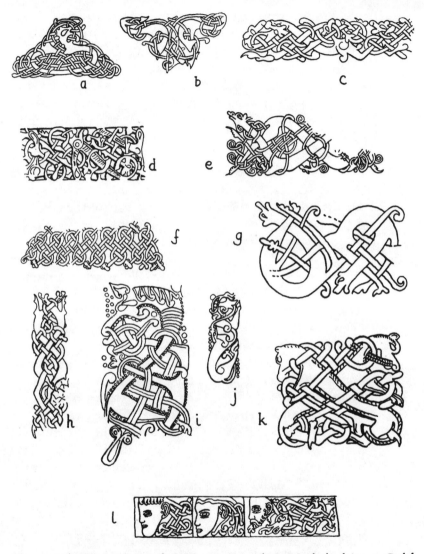

Fig. 34. *Irish Urnes patterns. a, b. Lismore crosier; c, d. St Manchan's shrine; e. Cashel sarcophagus; f. Dysert O Dea cross; g. Clonfert doorway; h. Glendalough cross; i, j. Tuam Cathedral east window; k. Kilmore doorway; l. Killeshin doorway. Not to scale.*

red, blue, and white, some of them in chequer patterns which may be an effort to reproduce the effect of millefiori. The crosier bears an inscription indicating that it was made about the year 1100.

Other pieces of metalwork from the south of Ireland show variants of the same style: the early twelfth-century shrine of St Lachtin's arm, from Freshford, Co. Kilkenny, engraved with interlaced animals; the Tau crosier (the only one of its kind to survive although crosiers of this form are fairly often depicted), also from Co. Kilkenny, with animal interlace and Ringerike scrolls; the engraved cast book-mounting from Holy Cross, Co. Tipperary, with the animal-combat theme; and there is a handsome crosier, not of metal but of ivory, from Aghadoe, Co. Kerry, which has a mixture of Urnes and Romanesque styles in its ornament. The shrine of the 'Bell of St Patrick's Will', with its openwork patterns of Urnes animals made by soldering together all the separate bronze elements of the design, was made in the north, probably in Armagh, between 1091 and 1105. It has filigree patterns almost as elaborately constructed as those of the Ardagh Chalice, but much coarser in texture.

But the two most splendid achievements of the Irish metal-workers in the Urnes style are from the west. The Cross of Cong, a large (2 feet 6 inches high) processional cross which was also a reliquary for a fragment of the True Cross, was commis-sioned by Toirdelbach Ua Conchubhair, king of Connacht, and was made about the year 1123. It is in the form of a large Latin cross made of sheets of bronze riveted together. Below the bottom of the shaft there is a handle projecting downward; the upper part of this is cast in the form of a large animal head which grips the bottom of the shaft in its jaws. Along the rims of the shaft and transom at intervals are projecting settings for enamel. The enamels used are red and yellow, one inlaid in the other in cruciform and step-patterns which seem to be a coarser imitation of the fine inlays of similar studs on such objects as

Plate 65

Plate 69

the Ardagh Chalice. Along the full length of the back of the shaft to the crossing, and again above the crossing and on the arms, openwork cast gilt-bronze panels are fitted against the plain bronze background of the inner casing. The openwork takes the form of a highly disciplined zoomorphic interlace which is almost perfectly symmetrical about the main axis. Similar interlace covers the front of the cross, where it is divided into panels. The theme of the interlace is the Urnes combat theme, robbed of the restless struggle it shows in Scandinavian work and reduced to an orderly pattern in which the contrast between the broad ribbon-bodies of the quadrupeds and the wiry bodies of the serpents rather than the mortal struggle of the creatures is emphasized. The work shows to perfection several constant features of Irish Urnes ornament: the combination of straight lines and sweeping curves, the regular figure-of-eight loopings of the serpents, and the profile-heads of the beasts, with rolled-back lower jaws, swelling snout with moustache-lappet, bulging brow, pointed ear, and pointed ovoid eye. On the front of the cross the serpents are depicted in the usual convention of the style, their heads shown as it were on plan, with projecting eyes and pointed ears. A large setting of rock-crystal is placed at the crossing in front, surrounded by spiral filigree, rather coarse in appearance as is usual at this date. The great stylized animal head, with ribbed snout and scaly brow, which grips the base of the cross, has little foliage patterns in the V of its gaping jaws.

A large bronze reliquary from Lemanaghan, Co. Offaly, St Manchan's shrine, which is obviously a variant of the house-shaped type of shrine but is made in the form of a gabled roof, has openwork binding strips and bosses with Urnes animal-ornament almost identical with that of the Cross of Cong, but slightly less coherent. It is probably a little later—perhaps five or ten years—in date. It has had added to it at some time not very long after it was made a number of curious little human

Plate 68

Fig. 35. A bronze figure mounted on St Manchan's shrine. Scale approximately ⅓.

Figs. 34c, 34d

figures cast in high relief in bronze in imitation of the Continental Romanesque crucifix-figures of the time.

With this piece the Irish metalworking tradition, at the height
of its renewed vigour, comes to a sudden end. When they
reverted to the old animal-themes in ornament in the mid-
eleventh century the Irish metalworkers had shown their conservatism and no doubt the conservatism of their monastic
patrons. But already at that time new ideas from the Continent
had begun to affect Irish affairs and a struggle between the new
and the old had begun in the monastic Church which was, as
ever, the chief patron of the metalworkers. That struggle ended
in the second quarter of the twelfth century with the triumph
of the innovators. Now the old monasteries themselves were in
their final decline, and the demand was not for the work of the
Irish bronzesmiths but for the mass-produced ecclesiastical
metalwork that was now available from Continental factories.
The enamelled crosier found at Cashel, made at Limoges in
the thirteenth century, has duplicates from the same mould at
Wells, Paris, Bonn, Munich, and elsewhere.

THE CHURCH REFORM

The Church in Ireland in the eleventh century, as in the seventh,
was organized, ruled, and administered by the monasteries
where the old rules were still observed; they were still walled
villages of huts and small churches. Their spirit, however, was
not that of the seventh century. Many of them had become rich
in land and they were ruled and the lands administered, according to ancient custom, by the *comharba* (successors) of the
founders. The office of *comharb* had become hereditary and was
often held by a layman. It was the presence now of Christian
Norse communities in the towns, who had no desire to have

their ecclesiastical affairs ruled by Irish *comharba*, and the effects
of the Gregorian reform on the Continent, which provided the
first impetus for ecclesiastical change in Ireland. From some
time early in the eleventh century Dublin sent priests to Canterbury to be consecrated as bishops. Waterford and Limerick
followed suit, and as a result the archbishops of Canterbury
began to take an interest in the Irish Church, even to claim
jurisdiction over it. St Anselm wrote in 1093 and 1103 to
Muirchertach Ua Briain, king of Munster (whom he addressed
as 'glorious king of Ireland'), urging him to look to the reform
of church affairs in Ireland, citing as abuses the dissolution of
marriages, the marriage of near relations, the irregular consecration of bishops, and the consecration of bishops without
regard to place and without fixed sees. Muirchertach was the
chief claimant of the high-kingship at the time and his life was
spent in almost constant warfare and in intrigues that were not
confined to Ireland but extended to Wales, where he en-
couraged the rebellion of Gerald the Steward against Henry I;
but he found time to take an interest in church affairs and he
had a native reformer to hand—Gilla Espuic, bishop of
Limerick, an Irishman who owed no allegiance to Canterbury. Muirchertach and Diarmait Ua Briain helped Gilla
Espuic organize a diocese of Limerick, and in 1101 Muirchertach, at a great assembly on the Rock of Cashel, made a grant
'such as no king had ever made before, namely he granted
Cashel of the kings to the Church',[1] thus setting up a rival, of   Plate 63
great and ancient prestige, to Emly, the chief monastery of
Munster. Other Irish churchmen, chief of whom were Cellach
of Armagh and Malchus of Lismore, were working to help
Gilla Espuic reform the Church, and in 1110 they achieved
their first triumph in the national synod convened at Rath
Bresail, near Cashel, and attended by Muirchertach and by
laity and clergy from many parts of the country. A new con-
stitution was drawn up for the Irish Church, providing for two

archbishops and twenty-four bishops with fixed sees and delimited dioceses. In this decision the influence of Canterbury is revealed, for the number of sees reflects (somewhat in-accurately) the organization planned for the English Church when Gregory II sent St Augustine to Kent in the sixth century.

The work of putting the proposed scheme into effect took another forty years, for the power of the vested interests in the Irish monasteries had to be overcome. Cellach of Armagh was now the spirit of the reform, and his right hand was St Malachy of Armagh, a young protégé whom he ordained, about the year 1119, and appointed his vicar, in which capacity Malachy reformed the diocese of Armagh, 'rooting out', in St Bernard's words, 'barbarous rites, to plant the rites of the Church'. Malachy also went south to Lismore to study for some time under Malchus and there he met, and seemingly converted to the ideals of the reform movement, Cormac Mac Carthaigh, soon to be king of Munster. Cellach himself was a member of one of the families of hereditary *comharba*, the Ui Shinaigh; when he died, Malachy succeeded him as *comharb* of Patrick and bishop of Armagh, but only after a long struggle with the Ui Shinaigh, in which he was aided by Ua Briain and Mac Carthaigh. Having succeeded, he immediately began to arrange for the convening of a new national synod at which the Pope's *pallia* could be distributed to new archbishops and the proposals of Rath Bresail finally put into effect. These arrange-ments took him twice to Rome, and on both journeys he stayed with St Bernard at Clairvaux, dying there on the way back from his second visit to the Pope. The synod he sought was convened four years after his death, at Kells in 1152, and the Pope's legate distributed *pallia* to four, not two, archbishops, of Armagh, Cashel, Tuam, and Dublin.

Meanwhile a shrewder blow than the establishment of dio-ceses had been struck at the hegemony of the old monasteries.

Malachy, departing homeward from Clairvaux after his first visit to Rome, had left some of his companions with St Bernard to be trained as novices in the Cistercian order in the hope that they might found a Cistercian house in Ireland. St Bernard wrote to Ireland to St Malachy in 1141, reporting on their progress and enjoining him to 'look out beforehand and prepare beforehand a place for them, like the places which you have seen here, apart from the commotions of the world'.[2] A secluded site on the southern borders of the then diocese oi Clogher was chosen; Donnchadh Ua Cerbhaill, king of Air-ghialla, gave the land, and in 1142 the Irishmen, together with some of St Bernard's monks, including his architect, came to begin the building of the abbey. It was finished in 1157 and an assembly of kings and bishops attended the consecration of the completed abbey church at Mellifont. It was of a type previously unknown in Ireland, a building two hundred feet long, not set in the midst of a cluster of cells, but part of the Cistercian complex of communal buildings; dormitories, refectory, chapter-house, cloister, cellars. And already by the date of its consecration a number of daughter-abbeys of Melli-font had been founded in Ireland. Already, too, the reformers had been bringing in the Canons Regular of St Augustine to take over some of the old monasteries; the Premonstratensians and the Franciscans, Dominicans, and other friars were to follow later, but it was the foundation of Mellifont that marked the end of the Irish monastic era.

THE LATE CROSSES

Only in stone-carving did something of the Irish tradition in art live on through the twelfth century, but in this too there were considerable changes. Some time in the eleventh century a new type of High Cross made its appearance in Ireland. In the graveyard at Killeany on the largest of the Aran Islands there are fragments of the shaft of a carved limestone cross. The carving is divided into panels, one of which depicts in a primitive convention a horseman wearing a short cape, another has the Ringerike foliate 'shell-spiral' motif; others have simple geometric patterns or more elaborate circular knotwork. This cross is the earliest of a coherent group, the products of a mason's workyard which flourished from the late eleventh century until the middle of the twelfth, extending from Aran across the sound to Kilfenora and Dysert O Dea on the main-land. All are carved of the local crystalline limestone and they share some minor ornamental motifs which are unknown elsewhere in Ireland but which suggest that the stone-carver who first began plying his trade in this desolate region had come from eastern Scotland. Remains of six crosses are known from the old monastic site at Kilfenora and three of them have figure-carving. All three are of almost slab-like proportion of thickness to width, and have relatively small cross-heads; these preserve the old ringed shape but are unpierced, and have stiff, crudely carved representations of the Crucifixion in bold relief occupying the upper half of one face of the shaft. Non-repre-sentational ornament tends to be on the upper part of the shaft, leaving it bare near the base, but one of the three, the 'Doorty cross', has an elaborate coarse animal interlace of degenerate Urnes form, below the feet of the Crucifixion and springing from the head of a horseman who seems to be galloping over a tiled or shingled roof. On the other main face of this cross a bishop is prominently carved on the upper part of the shaft, wearing a conical mitre, extending two fingers in blessing, and holding a crosier of Continental type; below him are two ecclesiastics, one holding a Tau crosier, the other a crosier of Irish type; and below them a bird of prey feeds on dismembered bodies. At Dysert O Dea the most prominent carvings are an even more stiffly carved Crucifixion, and another bishop, wearing a

Fig. 27

Plate 71

Plate 72

double-peaked mitre and holding a crosier of Continental type. Here there is a very varied ornament including straggling Urnes interlace and, on the base, an interlace of serpents with-out quadrupeds—a development that seems to have taken place in the Irish carvings in the Urnes style about the middle of the twelfth century. There is no reminiscence of the ringed form about the head of this cross, but there are surprising reversions to the old themes of the Scripture crosses in the carvings on the base: Daniel in the Den of Lions (though the lions have be-come interlaced Scandinavian monsters) and Adam and Eve.

Fig. 34f

At Tuam, Roscrea, Cashel, and Glendalough there are other crosses of the second quarter or the middle of the twelfth century, all with the same general characteristics; the prominent depiction of a bishop or the Crucifixion, the general absence of other figure-carving, and the extensive use of animal ornament in the Urnes style. Generally, in these late carvings, Christ is depicted with frontal gaze and clad in a long robe (perhaps under the influence of the cult of the *Volto Santo* of Lucca, as has been suggested), but at Glendalough the Late Romanesque and Gothic iconography appears; Christ is shown with inclined head and clad in a short kilt-like garment. A wedge-shaped sandstone tomb at Cashel also has its main face carved with elaborate Urnes ornament in relief; the pure combat-theme of the 'classic' period of the style, about A.D. 1130.

Fig. 34e

IRISH ROMANESQUE ARCHITECTURE

The late crosses are few in number compared with the Scrip-ture crosses, but by the middle of the twelfth century another medium had presented itself for the Irish stone-carvers. Cormac Mac Carthaigh, St Malachy's friend and ally in the Church reform movement, returned from Lismore as king of Munster to Cashel in 1127 and in the same year he had work begun on the building of a church on the Rock of Cashel which was probably thought of as a dramatic gesture like that by which Muirchertach Ua Briain had granted the Rock to the Church in 1101. Until then, churches in Ireland had continued to be unadorned simple rectangular buildings with pitched wooden roof-structures, although the addition of a small chancel, entered from the nave through a plain round arch, had become common. Cormac seems to have sent far and wide for masons to build his church; probably to Regensburg where a member of his family was bishop and whence two craftsmen had come to Cashel some years previously seeking funds for building; perhaps also to Hereford or Canterbury, where new cathedrals had just been built; perhaps to the north of England. Cormac's

Plate 70

Chapel was consecrated in 1134 and the contemporary accounts show that this was regarded as an event of considerable significance.

The chapel is a small church, of nave and square chancel, each with a steeply pitched stone roof containing a croft, and with square towers opening to the south and the north off the east end of the nave, built throughout of sandstone ashlar. There are no less than three richly ornamented doorways, one of them a full gabled porch, an elaborately carved chancel arch in four orders, many sculptured corbels, and, internally and externally, bands of blank arcading. The nave is barrel-vaulted, but the chancel is roofed by rib-vaulting, which at that date was a very advanced method of building. The internal wall-faces and the vault-spandrels of the chancel were thinly plastered and the plaster covered with paintings, of diapered ornament, figured scenes, and architectural compositions. The whole work is architectural, conceived in miniature in terms of a Romanesque cathedral of the time, but it is also richly ornamented with carvings; these vary from the naturalism of portrait-masks on the chancel arch to the grimacing grotesques

Fig. 36. Map showing remains of carved Romanesque churches (including fragments).

which are carved under the eaves in the nave. The ornament, in spite of its richness, however, is subordinated to the archi-tectural units—the full orders of impost, capital, shaft, and base —in the design.

This introduction of the Romanesque style had an im-mediate effect on Irish building, and Cormac's Chapel was widely imitated in the south-west of Ireland, especially in the Mac Carthaigh and Ua Briain territories. But the Irish masons, left to themselves, soon misunderstood and lost sight of most of the architectural features that had been introduced, and concentrated instead on elaboration of the ornament. The mouldings and one of the blank arcades are faithfully repro-duced in the earliest and closest imitation of Cormac's Chapel, the church at Kilmalkedar, Co. Kerry. Many of the details of the exterior arcades at Cashel are reproduced in blank arcading flanking the doorways of the cathedral at Ardfert, Co. Kerry, and St Cronan's church at Roscrea, Co. Tipperary. The deep gabled porch of the north doorway of Cashel was also imitated at Ardfert and Roscrea, but it soon became no longer a porch but an ornamented gable-shape simply carved on the wall-face, with its sloping sides tangential to the arch of a doorway below,

Plate 73

as at Clonfert Cathedral and the church at Killeshin, Co. Laois. The orders of doorways and chancel-arches, too, began to lose their architectural characteristics in the hands of Irish masons; capitals and bases lost their projection beyond the line of the shaft and lost also even the debased classical forms they had had at Cashel, being ornamented in ways that preserved nothing of their original function. This process can be traced in a number of small stone churches in Clare, Kerry, Limerick, and Tipperary which were built in the two decades following the erection of Cormac's Chapel.

At this stage the new fashion of building decorated churches

Fig. 36

became more widespread, and in the 1160's and '70's the series of ornamented churches which are generally recognized as

being in the typical 'Irish Romanesque' style were built, across
the full width of the midlands, the most notable examples being
the 'Nuns' Church' at Clonmacnoise, Clonfert Cathedral, the   Plate 76
two churches at Rahan, the churches at Killeshin, Mona
Incha, and Kilmore, and the cathedral of Tuam. A few Round
Towers of the period have doorways ornamented in similar
style.

The chief characteristic of these buildings, which archi-
tecturally are the same little wooden-roofed rectangular buildings with *antae* and sometimes with small chancels that had
long been erected in Ireland, is that the stone surfaces of doorways and chancel-arches are covered with a rich complex
surface-ornament, finely tooled in a graphic fashion often
hardly to be described as carving, and of a character which
would seem more appropriate in manuscript illumination than
in stone-sculpture. Animal interlacing of a debased Urnes   *Fig 34*
style appears on most of them; the chevron, adapted with
enthusiasm from Cormac's Chapel, appears in elaboration and
in great variety, often outlined with rows of small pellets which
strongly recall the dot-contouring of the early manuscripts;
bases are frequently bulbous forms retracted in under the
jambs; capitals are displaced by a frieze-like arrangement of
carved human heads with interlaced hair which assumes the
forms of struggling animals or foliate scrolls; the human head,
indeed, an old motif of Celtic art, is a frequent ornament, most
impressive in the strange ring of staring faces, with a few beak-   Plate 75
heads and cat-heads, on the arch of the doorway at Dysert
O Dea. Such ornament, although inappropriate, could be
most effective; the fine delicate web of lightly incised patterns
cast over the warm-coloured sandstone at Killeshin, or the   Plates 73, 74
barbaric richness of the carved doorway at Clonfert, are works
composed with the skilful balance that had been displayed in
the eighth-century manuscripts. But again in this late stone-
carving the Irish craftsmen had shown themselves unreceptive

to the changes of the time and had turned to the themes of the past. The last stages of Irish Romanesque, in the closing years of the twelfth century, show an increasing barbarism, with the Scandinavian monsters of the disintegrating Urnes style, in particular, destroying all architectural lines and crawling freely over all the members of such very late works as the Killaloe doorway. The influence of the severe architecture of the Cistercians did finally combine with the motifs of Irish Romanesque to produce in the early thirteenth century in the west a dignified and architectural Irish Transitional style, but by then it was too late to be more than a provincial phenomenon.

THE ANGLO-NORMAN INVASION

The church at Killeshin, which illustrates perhaps better than any other the characteristics of the Irish style, was built, about the year 1160, by Diarmait Mac Murchada, king of Leinster, a man who was a great founder of churches and who was also, even by the standards set by many of his colleagues of the time, a scoundrel. Yet the act for which he was to be execrated by generations of Irish writers was a perfectly normal and even respectable piece of policy. He had been driven from his kingdom in one of the incessant inter-provincial wars, and he fled across the Irish Sea to Britain. There, his chief concern being to recover his kingship of Leinster, he made a bargain with some adventurous knights in south Wales who agreed to help him in return for grants of land in Ireland. The first small contingent landed at Bannow Bay in Co. Wexford, defeated the Norse of Wexford who came out to drive them off, and entrenched themselves to await reinforcements. The main body arrived in 1169, took Wexford, Waterford, and Dublin, and within an astonishingly short time had over-run the midlands and were building motes-and-baileys to secure their conquered lands.

The Normans, in spite of their initial successes, never conquered Ireland. There was no tradition of allegiance to a central authority and the country could only be conquered *tuath* by *tuath*, but the invaders too soon became involved in the complexities of Irish alliances to accomplish this. In the cen-turies that followed, many of them became wholly absorbed into Irish society, abiding by Irish law and speaking the Irish language; only a thirty-mile-deep bridgehead around Dublin remained as a secure base for English law and custom in Ireland. But with the invasion the high-kingship, Irish monasticism, and Ireland's political and cultural isolation came to an end. It was the most drastic of the many changes that had taken place in the twelfth century.

As in the catastrophic sixteenth and seventeenth centuries, there was a great deal of compilation of old stories, verse, and traditions in the twelfth century. It was, in fact, the first great period of compilation and we owe much of our knowledge of early Irish literature to the manuscript miscellanies of this time. The language itself had been changing rapidly in the time of the Viking wars, and literary tastes changed; a new prose style came into being which bears about the same relation to Old Irish writing as does the more flamboyant rhetoric of the late Latin period to the work of Livy or Caesar—the change is illustrated by the two redactions of the old (mainly prose) epic, *Táin Bó Cuailgne*. Although the time produced many remarkable men, the literature of this period gives little evidence of a high quality of thought. There is elaboration and complexity in plenty—in the minutely detailed but quite unreal exposition of the rights and obligations of provincial kings in the *Book of Rights*, or in the absurd lives of the early saints which were written at this time—but it is sterile. All the revivals and reforms of the eleventh and twelfth centuries were not able to restore the life and form that Irish culture had had in the eighth century.

But the weaknesses in Irish society that became apparent in the period of change following the Viking wars were counter-balanced by strength, in decentralization, in the close intimate texture of family loyalties, and in tenacity and conservatism of character, which were to enable Ireland to survive further long centuries of warfare with much of her old social system intact. Ireland's culture from the coming of St Patrick until the Anglo-Norman invasion is the most illuminating example Europe has to offer of the development in literature, in art, in thought, and in the Christian religion, of a barbarian people who had remained outside the boundaries of the Roman Empire. It shows that without cities, without extensive commerce and communications, without central organization, without the State, something approaching civilization could flourish for a time. Equally, perhaps, it shows that such a state of things could not last indefinitely. But the full apparatus of the State did not come to Ireland until the sixteenth century. In the meantime something of the Early Christian way of life lived on; the Irish language, Irish law and custom, Irish literature. But it was an impoverished culture, struggling for its life. In spite of the literature, in spite of a revival of art, within the Gothic style, in the fifteenth and early sixteenth centuries, little is known of the society of the purely Irish parts of the country in that long period. Archaeology, so far, has nothing to tell of it, history little. It is clear, from what is revealed by the Elizabe-than writers who were engaged in the bloody conquest of the country in the late sixteenth century, that many things in the life of that hidden Ireland had remained unchanged since before the time of the Vikings. But what the Elizabethans described, they were sweeping away into the past.

Notes to Chapters

Numbers in parentheses refer to the Bibliography on p. 187

INTRODUCTION

1 Plummer (24), p. x.
2 Bede (64), Book I, Chap. 1.
3 Corkery (30), p. 188.

CHAPTER I

1 Tacitus, *Agricola*, Chap. 24.
2 Symmachus, *Epistola* II.
3 A good edition of the *Confessio* is to be found in White (62).
4 Haddan and Stubbs (41). Translation from Ryan (80), p. 97.

CHAPTER II

1 Reeves (63).
2 Murphy (78), p. 65.
3 Bede (64), Book III, Chap. 25.
4 Stokes (81), p. 26.
5 Leask (16), p. 1.
6 Bede (64), Book III, Chap. 5.
7 Bede (64), Book III, Chap. 27.
8 Translation from Greene (40), p. 88.
9 Flower (66), p. 42.
10 Murphy (78), p. 71.
11 Meyer, *Four Songs of Summer and Winter* (London, 1903), p. 14.
12 Murphy (78), p. 7.
13 Flower (66), p. 62.
14 Bede (64), Book III, Chap. 25.

CHAPTER III

1 Meyer (20), p. 110.
2 From the *Crith Gablach,* specially translated for this book by Professor David Greene.
3 Meyer, *Learning in Ireland in the Fifth Century* (Dublin, 1913), p. 19.
4 Murphy (78), p. 143.
5 Flower (66), p. 24.
6 Jackson (70), p. 136.
7 Translation from Dillon (88), p. 145.
8 Murphy (78), p. 15.
9 Murphy (78), p. 147.
10 Stokes (108).
11 Stokes (108).
12 Plummer (24), Vol. I, p. 107 (Vita Prima Sancti Brendani).
13 Murphy (78), p. 143.
14 Meyer, *The Triads of Ireland* (Dublin, 1906), p. 15.

CHAPTER IV

1 M. Masai in his book (126) on manuscript illumination would deny to Ireland virtually any part in the learning, art, and culture which we have described. His book was written during the war, when the evidence of the important pre-war excavations in Ireland was not available to him, but apart from this his argument is based

on many historical and other 'facts' which are demonstrably false. The reader is referred to items 79, 118, 129 in our Bibliography.

2 From a letter of St Columbanus to Pope Gregory the Great, A.D. 600. Quoted in Kenny (15), p. 191.

3 Translated by Liam de Paor from *The Oxford Book of Mediaeval Latin Verse* (ed. Stephen Gaselee), Oxford, 1928.

CHAPTER V

1 Todd (158), p. 51.
2 Carney (142), p. 75.
3 Todd (158), p. 41.
4 Bøe (141), p. 34.

5 Giraldus (145).
6 Todd (158), p. 79.
7 Translation from Shetelig (26), Vol. I, p. 56.
8 St Boniface, *Epistolae*, translation from Kenny (15), p. 524.
9 Hericus Autissiodorensis, *Epistola dedicatoria ad Carolum Calvum*, translation from Kenny (15), p. 593.
10 Henry (11), p. 108.
11 Henry (11), p. 168.
12 Jackson (70), p. 148.

CHAPTER VI

1 Four Masters (1), sub anno 1101.
2 Lawlor (172), p. 132.

Bibliography

The items in the select bibliography which follows are arranged for convenience under the chapters to which they are most relevant. In many cases, however, works listed under one chapter heading may be of use with reference to other chapters also. More extensive bibliographies are to be found in Nos. 10 and 25 listed below. The following abbreviations are used:

Ant. J.   *The Antiquaries Journal*

J C H A S   *Journal of the Cork Historical and Archaeological Society*

J G A H S   *Journal of the Galway Archaeological and Historical Society*

J R S A I   *Journal of the Royal Society of Antiquaries of Ireland*

P R I A   *Proceedings of the Royal Irish Academy*

P S A S   *Proceedings of the Society of Antiquaries of Scotland*

R S A I   Royal Society of Antiquaries of Ireland

U J A   *Ulster Journal of Archaeology*

General

(1) *Annals of the Kingdom of Ireland by the Four Masters* (ed. John O'Donovan), Dublin, 1848–51. (2) *Annals of Ulster* (ed. W. M. Hennessey and B. McCarthy), Dublin, 1887–1901. (3) *Annals of Inisfallen* (ed. Seán Mac Airt), Dublin, 1951. (4) BRØNDSTED, J. *Early English Ornament*, London and Copenhagen, 1924. (5) CARNEY, JAMES *Studies in Irish Literature and History*, Dublin, 1955. (6) CRAWFORD, HENRY S. *Handbook of Carved Ornament of the Early Christian Period*, Dublin, 1926. (7) CRUDEN, STEWART *The Early Christian and Pictish Monuments of Scotland*, Edinburgh, 1957. (8) DILLON, MYLES (ed.) *Early Irish Society*, Dublin, 1954. (9) HARDEN, D. B. (ed.) *Dark Age Britain*, London, 1956. (10) HENRY, FRANÇOISE *La Sculpture Irlandaise pendant les douze premiers siècles de l'ère chrétienne*, 2 vols., Paris, 1933; (11) *Irish Art*

in the Early Christian Period, London, 1940; (12) *Early Christian Irish Art,* Dublin, 1954. (13) JOYCE, P. W. *A Social History of Ancient Ireland,* 2 vols., London, New York and Bombay, 1903. (14) KENDRICK, T. D. *Anglo-Saxon Art,* London, 1938. (15) KENNEY, JAMES F. *The Sources for the Early History of Ireland,* vol. 1, New York, 1929. (16) LEASK, H. G. *Irish Churches and Monastic Buildings,* Dundalk, 1955. (17) MACALISTER, R. A. S. *The Archaeology of Ireland,* London, 1928. (18) MACNEILL, EOIN *Phases of Irish History,* Dublin, 1937. (19) MAHR, ADOLF (ed.) *Christian Art in Ancient Ireland,* vol. 1, Dublin, 1932. (20) MEYER, KUNO *Selections from Ancient Irish Poetry,* Constable's Miscellany, London, 1928. (21) O'RAHILLY, T. F. *Early Irish History and Mythology,* Dublin, 1946. (22) Ó RÍORDÁIN, SEÁN P. *Antiquities of the Irish Countryside,* Cork, 1942; London, 1953. (23) PETRIE, GEORGE *Christian Inscriptions in the Irish Language* (ed. Margaret Stokes) 2 vols., Dublin, 1872, 1878. (24) PLUMMER, C. *Vitae Sanctorum Hiberniae,* Oxford, 1910. (25) RAFTERY, JOSEPH (ed.) *Christian Art in Ancient Ireland,* vol. II, Dublin, 1941. (26) SHETELIG, HAAKON (ed.) *Viking Antiquities in Great Britain and Ireland,* vols. I–VI, Oslo, 1940–54. (27) SMITH, REGINALD *British Museum Anglo-Saxon Guide,* London, 1923. (28) STOKES, MARGARET *Early Christian Art in Ireland,* London, 1887 and Dublin, 1911, 1928. (29) WAINWRIGHT, F. T. (ed.) *The Problem of the Picts,* Nelson, 1955.

Introduction

(30) CORKERY, DANIEL *The Hidden Ireland,* Dublin, 1941.

Chapter One

(31) BIELER, LUDWIG *The Life and Legend of St Patrick,* Dublin, 1949. (32) BRUCE-MITFORD, R. L. S. *The Sutton Hoo Ship Burial,* British Museum Guide, London, 1947; (33) 'The Sutton Hoo Ship-Burial', *Proceedings of the Suffolk Inst. of Arch.,* 25, 1949. (34) BURY, J. B. *The Life of St Patrick and His Place in History,* London, 1905. (35) CLAPHAM,

A. W. 'Notes on the Origins of Hiberno-Saxon Art', *Antiquity*, 8 (1934), 43. (36) DANIEL, GLYN E. 'Who Are the Welsh?', *Proc. British Academy*, 40. (37) DILLON, MYLES *Cycles of the Kings*, Oxford, 1946. (38) ESPOSITO, MARIO 'The Patrician Problem and a possible solution', *Irish Historical Studies*, 10 (1956), 131. (39) EXNER, K. 'Die provinzialrömischen Emailfibeln der Rheinlande', 29th *Bericht der Römisch-Germanischen Kommission*, Berlin, 1939. (40) GREENE, DAVID 'Early Irish Society', in *Early Irish Society*, ed. Myles Dillon, Dublin, 1945. (41) HADDAN and STUBBS *Councils and Ecclesiastical Documents relating to Great Britain and Ireland*, Oxford, 1869–78. (42) HENRY, FRANÇOISE 'Emailleurs d'Occident', *Préhistoire*, Tome II, fasc. I, p. 65, Paris, 1933; (43) 'Hanging-Bowls', *J R S A I*, 66 (1936), 209; (44) 'Irish Enamels of the Dark Ages and the Cloisonné Techniques', in *Dark Age Britain*, London, 1956 (ed. D. B. Harden). (45) KENDRICK, T. D. 'British Hanging-Bowls', *Antiquity*, 6 (1932), 161. (46) KILBRIDE-JONES, H. E. 'The Evolution of Penannular Brooches with Zoomorphic Terminals in Great Britain and Ireland', *P R I A*, 43C (1937), 379. (47) LEEDS, E. T. *Celtic Ornament*, Oxford, 1933; (48) *Early Anglo-Saxon Art and Archaeology*, Oxford, 1935. (49) LEISTÖL, ASLAK 'The Hanging Bowl, A Liturgical and Domestic Vessel', *Acta Archaeologica*, 24 (1953), 163. (50) MACALISTER, R. A. S. 'On Some Antiquities Discovered upon Lambay', *P R I A*, 38 (1929), 240. (51) O'KELLY, M. J. 'Excavation of a Ring-fort at Garryduff, Co. Cork' (Preliminary Report), *Antiquity*, 20 (1946), 122. (52) O'RAHILLY, T. F. *The Two Patricks*, Dublin, 1942. (53) Ó RÍORDÁIN, SEÁN P. 'The Excavation of a Large Earthen Ring-Fort at Garranes, Co. Cork', *P R I A*, 47C (1942), 77; (54) 'Roman Material in Ireland', *P R I A*, 51C (1947), 35; (55) *Tara: the Monuments on the Hill*, Dundalk, 1954. (56) Ó RÍORDÁIN, SEÁN P. and HARTNETT, P. J. 'The Excavation of Ballycatteen Fort, Co. Cork', *P R I A*, 49C (1943), I. (57) POWELL, T. G. E. *The Celts*, London, 1958. (58) RAFTERY, J. *Prehistoric Ireland*, London, 1951. (59) RIEGL, A. *Spätrömische Kunstindustrie* (2nd ed.), Vienna, 1927. (60) SMITH, REGINALD 'The Evolution of the Hand-pin in Great Britain and Ireland', *Opuscula Archaeologica Oscari Montelio Septuagenario Dicata*, Stockholm, 1913, p. 281; (61) *British Museum Iron Age Guide*, London, 1925. (62) WHITE, NEWPORT J. D. 'Libri Sancti Patricii: the Latin Writings of St Patrick', *P R I A*, 25C (1905), 201–36.

Chapter Two

(63) ADAMNÁN (see Reeves) *Life of St Columba.* (64) BEDE, THE VENERABLE *Historia Ecclesiastica gentis Anglorum.* (65) DE PAOR, LIAM 'A Survey of Sceilg Mhichíl', *J R S A I*, 85 (1955), 174. (66) FLOWER, ROBIN *The Irish Tradition*, Oxford, 1947. (67) GOUGAUD, DOM LOUIS *Christianity in Celtic Lands,* London, 1932. (68) HENRY, FRANÇOISE 'Early Monasteries, Beehive Huts, and Dry-Stone Houses in the Neighbourhood of Caherciveen and Waterville (Co. Kerry)', *P R I A,* 58C (1957), 45. (69) JACKSON, KENNETH 'Notes on the Ogam Inscriptions of Southern Britain', *The Early Cultures of North-west Europe* (ed. Cyril Fox and Bruce Dickins), Cambridge, 1950, p. 199; (70) *A Celtic Miscellany*, 1951. (71) KENDRICK, T. D. 'Gallen Priory Excavations 1934-5', *J R S A I*, 69 (1939), 1. (72) LAWLOR, H. C. *The Monastery of Saint Mochaoi of Nendrum*, Belfast, 1925. (73) LEASK, H. G. *Glendalough, Co. Wicklow* (Official Guide), Dublin, 1951. (74) MACALISTER, R. A. S. *The Memorial Slabs of Clonmacnois*, R S A I Extra Volume, Dublin, 1909; (75) *Corpus Inscriptionum Insularum Celticarum*, 2 vols. Dublin, 1945, 1949. (76) MURPHY, GERARD *The Ossianic Lore and Romantic Tales of Medieval Ireland*, Dublin, 1955; (77) *Saga and Myth in Ancient Ireland*, Dublin, 1955; (78) *Early Irish Lyrics*, Oxford, 1956. (63) REEVES, WILLIAM (ed.) *Saint Adamnan, Abbot of Hy, Life of St Columba, Founder of Hy*, Edinburgh, 1874. (79) RYAN, JOHN 'Irish Learning in the Seventh Century', *J R S A I*, 80 (1950), 164; (80) *Irish Monasticism, Origins and early development*, Dublin, 1931. (81) STOKES, WHITLEY (ed.) *Féilire Oengusso,* Henry Bradshaw Society, vol. XXIX, London, 1905. (82) WARREN, F. E. (ed.) *The Antiphonary of Bangor,* Henry Bradshaw Society, vol. IV, London, 1893.

Chapter Three

(83) BERSU, GERHARD 'Three Celtic Homesteads in the Isle of Man', *Journal Manx Museum*, 5 (1945-6), 177; (84) 'The Rath in Townland Lissue, Co. Antrim', *U J A*, 10 (1947), 30. (85) BINCHY, D. A. *Críth Gablach*, Dublin, 1941; (86) 'Secular Institutions', in *Early Irish Society* ed. Myles Dillon, Dublin, 1954. (87) COLLINS, A. E. P. 'Excavations at Lough Faughan Crannog', *UJA*, 18 (1955), 45. (88) DILLON,

MYLES *Early Irish Literature*, Chicago, 1948. (89) DUIGNAN, MICHAEL 'Irish Agriculture in Early Historic Times', *J R S A I*, 74 (1944), 124. (90) HENCKEN, HUGH 'Ballinderry Crannog No. 1', *P R I A*, 43 (1936), 103; (91) *Cahercommaun, A Stone Fort in Co. Clare*, R S A I Extra Volume, 1938; (92) 'Ballinderry Crannog No. 2', *P R I A*, 47 (1942), 1; (93) 'Lagore Crannog, an Irish Royal Residence of the 7th to 10th Centuries A.D.', *P R I A*, 53 (1950), 1. (94) HENRY, FRANÇOISE 'Habitation Sites on Inishkea North, Co. Mayo', *J R S A I*, 77 (1947), 39; (95) 'A Wooden Hut on Inishkea North, Co. Mayo', *J R S A I*, 82 (1952), 163. (96) MCCLINTOCK, H. F. *Old Irish and Highland Dress*, Dundalk, 1950. (97) MACNEILL, EOIN 'Ancient Irish Law. The Law of Status and Franchise', *P R I A*, 36C (1921–4). (98) MACWHITE, EOIN 'Early Irish Board Games', *Éigse*, 5 (1945–7), 25. (99) O'KELLY, M. J. 'St Gobnet's House, Ballyvourney, Co. Cork', *J C H A S*, 57 (1952), 18; (100) 'Excavations and Experiments in Ancient Irish Cooking-Places', *J R S A I*, 84 (1954), 105; (101) 'An Island Settlement at Beginish, Co. Kerry', *P R I A*, 57C (1956), 159. (102) Ó RÍORDÁIN, SEÁN P. 'Lough Gur Excavations: Carraig Aille and the Spectacles', *P R I A*, 52C (1949), 39; (103) 'Excavation of Some Earthworks on the Curragh', *P R I A*, 53C (1950), 249. (104) Ó RÍORDÁIN, SEÁN P. and FOY, J. B. 'The Excavation of Leacanabuaile Stone Fort near Caherciveen, Co. Kerry', *J C H A S*, 46 (1941), 85. (105) Ó RÍORDÁIN, SEÁN P. and MACDERMOTT, M. 'Excavation of a Ring-Fort at Letterkeen, Co. Mayo', *P R I A*, 54 (1952), 89. (106) SHAW, FRANCIS Summary of literary evidence for the Irish House, *Archaeological News Letter*, January 1952, p. 73. (107) SHAW, FRANCIS Chapter in McClintock, *Old Irish and Highland Dress*, Dundalk, 1950. (108) STOKES, WHITLEY (ed.) *Cormac's Glossary*, 1886. (109) WATER-MAN, D. M. 'The Excavation of a House and Souterrain at White Fort, Drumaroad, Co. Down', *U J A*, 19 (1956), 73; (110) 'The Excavation of a House and Souterrain at Craig Hill, Co. Antrim', *U J A*, 19 (1956), 87.

Chapter Four

(111) ÅBERG, N. *The Occident and the Orient in the Art of the Seventh Century*, vols. I–III, Stockholm, 1943–7. (112) *Book of Kells* Facsimile

Edition, 3 vols., Bern, 1950-1. (113) COFFEY, G. *Guide to the Celtic
Antiquities of the Christian Period*, Dublin, 1909. (114) COLLING-
WOOD, W. G. *Northumbrian Crosses of the Pre-Norman Age*, London,
1927. (115) CURLE, C. M. 'The Chronology of the Early Chris-
tian Monuments of Scotland', *P S A S*, 74 (1939-40), 60. (116)
DUIGNAN, MICHAEL 'The Moylough (Co. Sligo) and other Irish
Belt-Reliquaries', *J G A H S*, 24 (1951), 83. (117) FRIEND, A. M.
'The Canon Tables of the Book of Kells', *Medieval Studies in Memory of
A. Kingsley Porter*, Cambridge (Mass.), vol. 1, 1939, p. 611. (118)
HENRY, FRANÇOISE 'Deux objets de bronze irlandais au Musée des
Antiquités nationales', *Préhistoire*, 1938, p. 65; (119) 'Irish Culture in
the Seventh Century', *Studies*, 1948, p. 267; (120) 'Les débuts de la
miniature irlandaise', *Gazette des Beaux-Arts*, 1950, p. 5. (121) HOLM-
QVIST, WILHELM *Germanic Art during the first millennium A.D.*, Stockholm, 1955; (122) 'An Irish Crozier-head Found near Stockholm',
Ant. J. 35 (1955), 46. (123) HUNT, JOHN 'On Two "D"-shaped
objects in the St Germain Museum', *P R I A*, 57C (1956), 153.
(124) *Lindisfarne Gospels* Facsimile Edition, 2 vols., Bern, 1956, 1960.
(125) LOWE, E. A. *Codices latini antiquiores*, vols. I-III, Oxford, 1934,
1935, 1938. (126) MASAI, F. *Essai sur les origines de la miniature dite
irlandaise*, Brussels, 1947. (127) MICHELI, GENEVIÈVE *L'Eluminure du
Haut Moyen-Age et les influences Irlandaises'*, Brussels, 1939. (128) NORDEN-
FALK, CARL 'Before the Book of Durrow', *Acta Archaeologica*, 18 (1947),
141. (129) Ó RÍORDÁIN, SEÁN P. 'The Genesis of the Celtic Cross',
Féilscríbhinn Torna, Cork, 1947, p. 108; (130) 'Notes on the Archaeological Evidence', *Studies*, 1948, p. 275. (131) PETERSEN, JAN *British
Antiquities of the Viking Period found in Norway*, vol. v of *Viking Antiquities
in Great Britain and Ireland*, Oslo, 1940. (132) *St Gall: Irish Miniatures
of the Foundation Library in St Gall*, Facsimile, Bern, 1953. (133) SMITH,
REGINALD 'Irish Brooches of Five Centuries', *Archaeologia*, 65 (1913-
14), 223. (134) STEVENSON, R. B. K. 'Pictish Art', in *The Problem of
the Picts*, Nelson, 1955, p. 97; (135) 'The Chronology and Relationship
of some Irish and Scottish Crosses', *J R S A I*, 86 (1956), 84. (136)
SULLIVAN, E. *The Book of Kells, described and illustrated*, London, 1914.
(137) SWARZENSKI, G. 'An Early Anglo-Irish Portable Shrine',
Bulletin of the Museum of Fine Arts, Boston, October 1954, p. 50. (138)
WILSON, DAVID M. 'An Irish Mounting in the National Museum,

Copenhagen', *Acta Archaeológica,* 26 (1955), 163. (139) ZIMMERMAN, E. HEINRICH *Vorkarolingische Miniaturen,* Berlin, 1916.

Chapter Five

(140) BØE, JOHS 'An Ornamented Bronze Object found in a Norwegian Grave', *Bergens Museums Aarbok,* 1924–5; (141) *Norse Antiquities in Ireland,* vol. III of *Viking Antiquities in Great Britain and Ireland,* Oslo, 1940. (142) CARNEY, JAMES 'The Impact of Christianity', in *Early Irish Society* ed. Dillon, Dublin, 1954. (143) COFFEY, G. and ARMSTRONG 'Scandinavian Objects found at Islandbridge and Kilmainham', *P R I A,* 28C (1910), 107. (144) FLOWER, ROBIN 'Irish High Crosses', *Journal of the Warburg and Courtauld Institutes,* vol. XVII; nos. 1–2, 1954, p. 87. (145) GIRALDUS CAMBRENSIS *Topographia Hibernica,* translated by John J. O'Meara, Dundalk, 1951: *Topography of Ireland by Giraldus Cambrensis.* (146) HALLIDAY, C. *The Scandinavian Kingdom of Dublin,* Dublin, 1884. (147) HENRY, FRANÇOISE 'L'Inscription de Bealin', *Revue Archéologique,* 1930, p. 111. (148) KENDRICK, T. D. *A History of the Vikings,* London, 1930. (149) MACALISTER, R. A. S. *Monasterboice,* Dundalk, 1946. (150) MAC DERMOTT, MÁIRE 'The Kells Crosier', *Archaeologia,* 96 (1955), 59–113; (151) 'The Crosiers of St Dympna and St Mel and Tenth Century Irish Metalwork', *P R I A,* 58C (1957), 167. (152) Ó RÍORDÁIN, SEÁN P. 'Recent Acquisitions from Co. Donegal in the National Museum', *P R I A,* 42C (1935), 180. (153) PETERSSON, BRITA ALENSTRAM 'Irish Imports into South Sweden', *Bulletin de la Société Royale des Lettres de Lund,* 1951–2, p. 233. (154) PETRIE, GEORGE *The Ecclesiastical Architecture of Ireland anterior to the Norman Invasion,* Dublin, 1845. (155) PORTER, ARTHUR KINGSLEY *The Crosses and Culture of Ireland,* New Haven, 1931. (156) SEXTON, ERIC H. L. *Irish Figure Sculptures,* Portland, Maine, 1946. (157) SHETELIG, HAAKON 'The Viking Graves in Great Britain and Ireland', *Acta Archaeologica,* 16 (1945), 1. (158) TODD, J. H. (ed. and translated) *The Wars of the Gaedhil with the Gaill, or the Invasion of Ireland by the Danes and Other Norsemen,* Rolls Series, London, 1867. (159) WADDELL, HELEN *The Wandering Scholars,* Pelican Books, 1954. (160) WALSH, A. *Scandinavian Relations with Ireland,* Dublin, 1922. (161) WHEELER, R. E. M. *London and the Vikings,* London, 1927.

Chapter Six

(162) ÅBERG, N. *Keltiska och orientaliska stilinflytelser i vikingatidens nordiska konst,* Stockholm, 1941. (163) CHAMPNEYS, A. C. *Irish Ecclesiastical Architecture,* London, 1910. (164) CLAPHAM, A. W. *English Romanesque Architecture before the Conquest,* Oxford, 1930; (165) *Romanesque Architecture of Western Europe,* Oxford, 1936. (166) DE PAOR, LIAM 'The Limestone Crosses of Clare and Aran', *J G A H S* 26 (1956), 53. (167) DUNRAVEN, EARL OF *Notes on Irish Architecture* (ed. Margaret Stokes), 2 vols., London, 1875, 1877. (168) HOLMQVIST, WILHELM 'Viking Art in the Eleventh Century', *Acta Archaeologica,* 22 (1951), 1. (169) KENDRICK, T. D. and SENIOR, ELIZABETH 'St Manchan's Shrine', *Archaeologia,* 86 (1937), 105. (170) KENDRICK, T. D. *Late Saxon and Viking Art,* London, 1949. (171) KERMODE, P. M. C. *Manx Crosses,* London, 1907. (172) LAWLOR, H. J. *St Bernard of Clairvaux's Life of St Malachy of Armagh,* London and New York, 1920. (173) MOE, OLE HENRIK 'Urnes and the British Isles. A Study of Western Impulses in Nordic Styles of the 11th Century', *Acta Archaeologica,* 26 (1955), 1. (174) O'SULLIVAN, WILLIAM 'The Earliest Irish Coinage', *J R S A I,* 79 (1949), 190. (175) SHETELIG, HAAKON 'Stil og tidsbestemmelser i de nordiske korsene paa øen Man', *Opuscula Archaeologica Oscari Montelio Septuagenario Dictata,* Stockholm, 1918, p. 391; (176) 'The Norse Style of Ornamentation in the Viking Settlements', *Acta Archaeologica,* 19 (1948), 69.

Supplement for the Fourth Impression

General: CHADWICK, N. K. *Celtic Britain,* London, 1963. Chapter One: BINCHY, D. A., 'Patrick and his Biographers: Ancient and Modern', *Studia Hibernica,* 2 (1962), 7; CARNEY, JAMES, *The Problem of St Patrick,* Dublin, 1961. Chapter Two: ANDERSON, A. O. and M. O. *Adomnan's Life of Columba,* London, 1961; CHADWICK, N. K., *The Age of the Saints in the Early Celtic Church,* London, 1961. Chapter Three: O'KELLY, M. J. 'Two Ring Forts at Garryduff, Co. Cork', *P R I A,* 63c (1962), 17. Chapter Four: O'DELL, A. C. *et al.,* 'The St Ninian's Isle Silver Hoard', *Antiquity,* 33 (1959), 241; WILSON, D. M., *The Anglo-Saxons,* London, 1960; *Book of Durrow,* Facsimile Edition, 2 vols., Bern, 1960. Chapter Five: ARBMAN, H., *The Vikings,* London, 1961.

List of Manuscripts mentioned in text

Book of Durrow—Trinity College Library, 57, Dublin. Book of Kells—Trinity College Library, 58, Dublin. *Cathach* of St Columba—Royal Irish Academy Library, S.N.1, Dublin. Codex Ambrosianus, D.23 Sup., Ambrosian Library, Milan. Codex Amiatinus, Biblioteca Laurenziana, Florence. Codex Usserianus Primus, Trinity College Library, 55, Dublin. Cuthbert Gospels, National Library, 1224 (Salisb. 32), Vienna. Dioskorides manuscript—Vienna. Durham Gospel fragment—A. 11. 10, Cathedral Library, Durham. Leningrad Gospels—F.V.I.N.8, now in State Public Library, Moscow. Lichfield Gospel—Gospel of St Chad, Cathedral Library, Lichfield. Lindisfarne Gospels—British Museum, Cotton Nero D. IV, London. Mac Regol—3946 Auct.D. II. 19, Bodleian Library, Oxford. Maihingen Gospel—1, 2, Collection Ottingen–Wallerstein, Maihingen. Priscian Grammar—B.P.L.67, University Library, Leyden. St Gall Gospels—Codex 51, Cathedral Library, St Gall. St Gall, Priscian Grammar, 904, Cathedral Library, St Gall. Thomas Evangeliar—Cathedral Library, Trier.

Sources of Illustrations

Original photographs for the plates were supplied by the Commissioners of Public Works in Ireland, 6–10, 12–14, 22, 23, 25–7, 36, 38, 51–7, 63, 70–6; Bórd Fáilte Éireann, 1–3, 16, 19–21, 24, 29–31, 37, 62, 64, 66–9; National Museum of Ireland, 4, 5, 28, 39–41, 46–50, 61, 65; Department of Archaeology, University College, Dublin, 18, 32–5; Trustees of the British Museum, 58–60; Universitetets Oldsaksamling Oslo, 43–5; Videnskapselskapets Oldsaksamling Trondheim, 42; Cork Public Museum, 17; Aerofilms, 11; J. K. St Joseph, Committee of Aerial Photography, University of Cambridge by permission of the Air Ministry (Crown Copyright reserved), 15.

All the drawings for the figures, with the exception of figures 29 and 32, are by Liam de Paor. The drawings for figure 29 by Máire de Paor and for figure 32 by Mrs Gabriel Ó Ríordáin are reproduced by courtesy of the Society of Antiquaries of London.

All the objects are preserved in the National Museum of Ireland, Dublin, unless otherwise stated.

Sources of Quotations

We have quoted from the following works by kind permission of the Publishers. Detailed references are supplied in the Notes to Chapters, p. 185, and in the Bibliography: Corkery, *The Hidden Ireland*, M. H. Gill and Son; Murphy, *Early Irish Lyrics*, Clarendon Press; Flower, *The Irish Tradition*, Clarendon Press; Jackson, *A Celtic Miscellany*, Routledge and Kegan Paul; Dillon, *Early Irish Literature*, University of Chicago Press; Meyer, *Four Songs of Summer and Winter*, D. Nutt; Meyer, *Learning in Ireland in the Fifth Century*, Hodges, Figgis; Meyer, *The Triads of Ireland* (Todd Lecture Series No. XIII), Royal Irish Academy; Meyer, *Selections from Ancient Irish Poetry*, Constable.

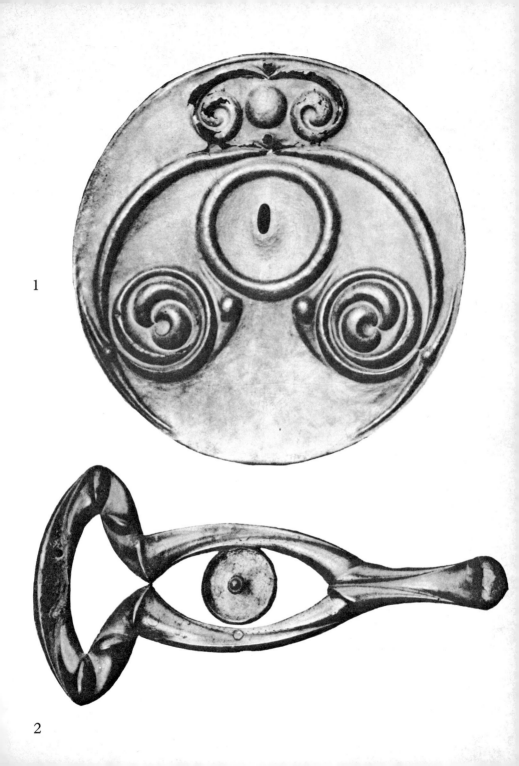

1

2

3

4

5

7

11

12

13

14

17

18

20

21

22

23

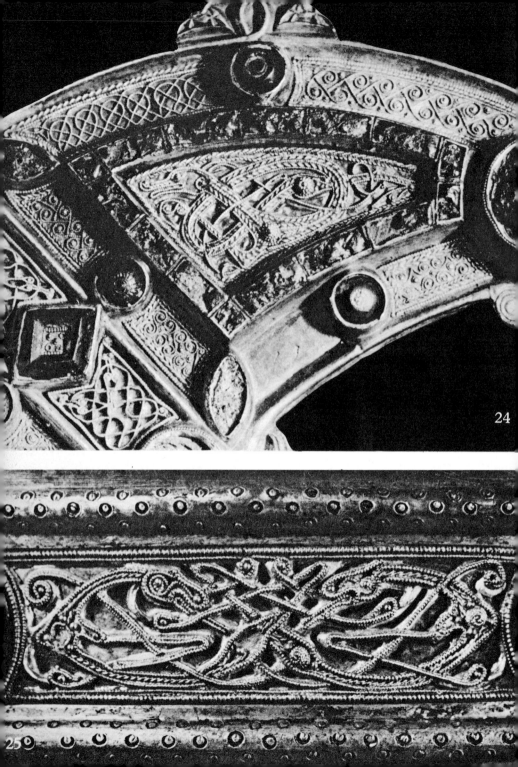

24

25

26

28

29

0

31

33

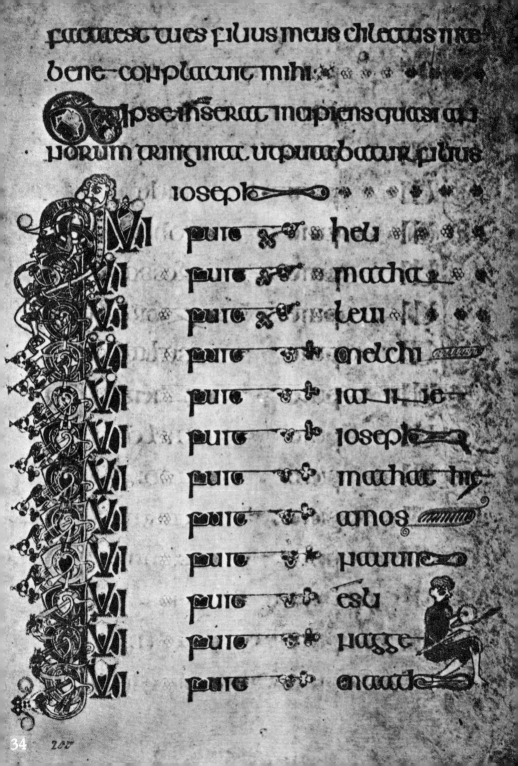

factus est dies filius meus dilectus in te

bene complacuit mihi

Ipse ihs erat incipiens quasi an

norum triginta ut putabatur filius

ioseph

qui fuit heli

qui fuit mathat

qui fuit leui

qui fuit melchi

qui fuit iannæ

qui fuit ioseph

qui fuit mathat hic

qui fuit amos

qui fuit naum

qui fuit esli

qui fuit nagge

qui fuit enaad

36

38

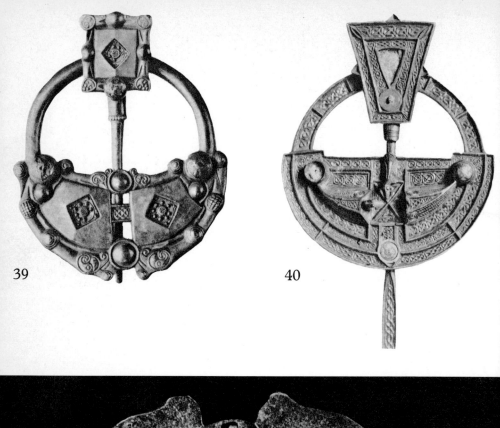

39   40

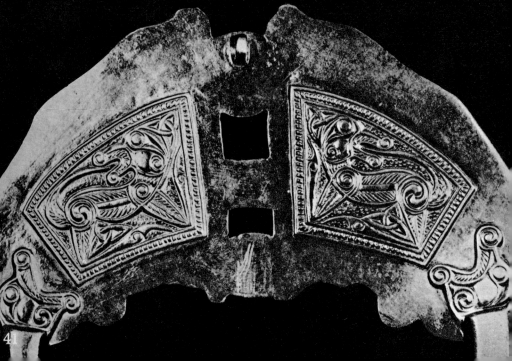

41

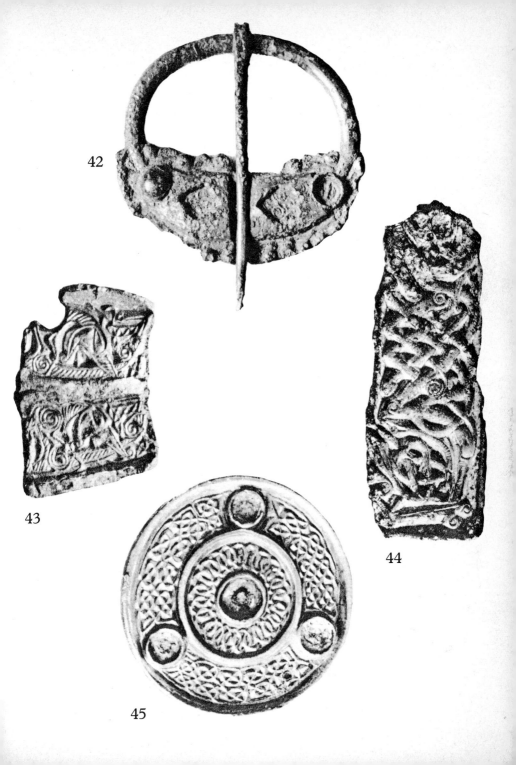

42

43

44

45

46

47

48

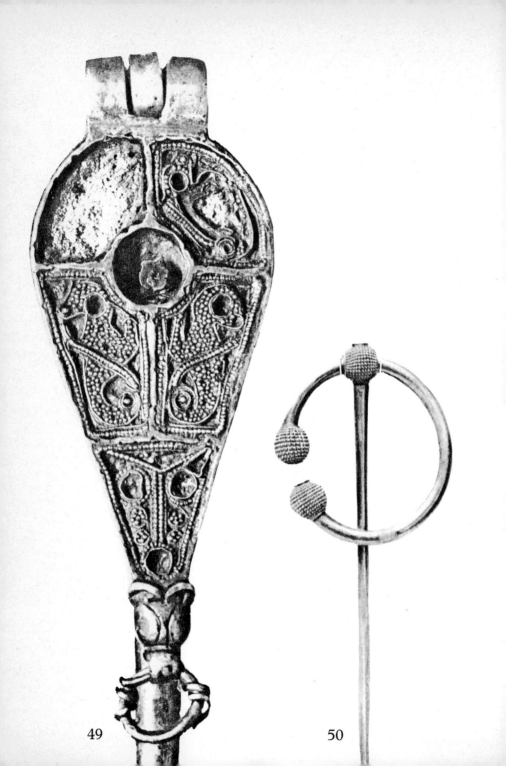

49   50

51

52

53

54

55

56

57

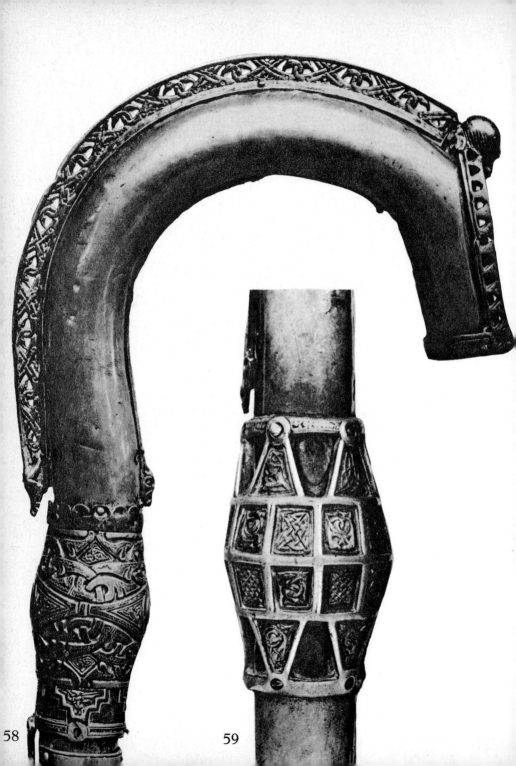

58   59

60

61

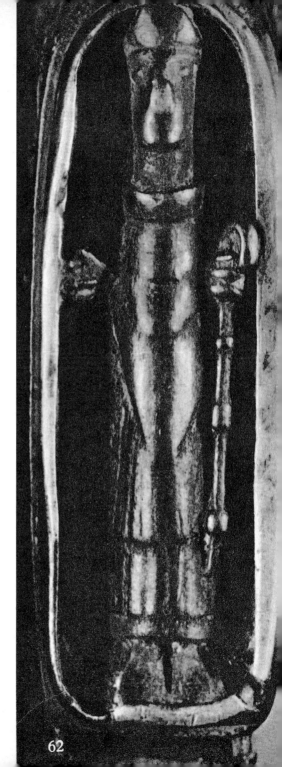

62

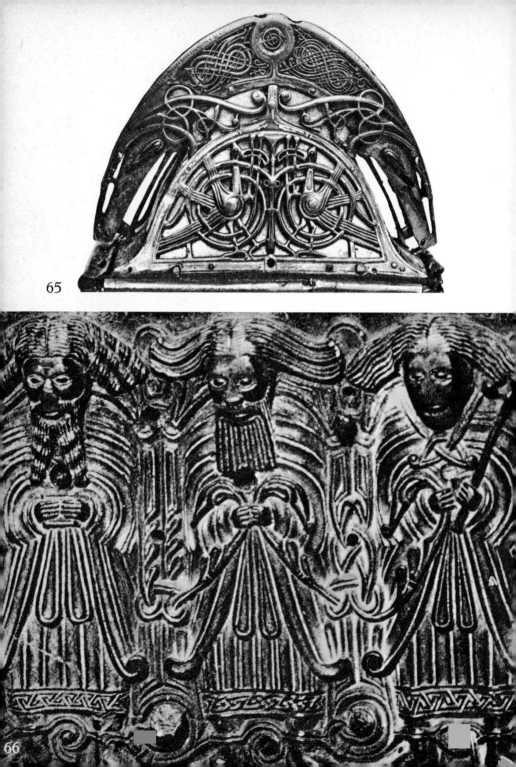

65

66

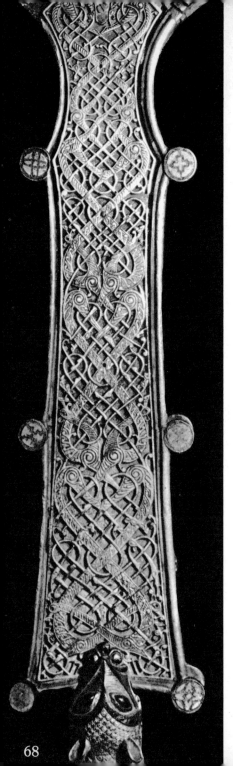

68

69

71

73

74

75

76

NOTES ON THE PLATES

Notes on the Plates

Abbreviation: N M I—National Museum of Ireland

1 Bronze disc with repoussé ornament in La Tène style. From a bog at Monasterevin, Co. Kildare. A number of such discs has been found in Ireland but their purpose is unknown. Diameter 12 in. Early Iron Age, second century A.D. N M I

2 Fibula of bronze with plastic ornament. From Emain Macha (Navan Fort, Co. Armagh), the royal site of the Ulaid, a place which is of importance in the earliest Irish saga-literature. About 4½ in. long. Early Iron Age, second century A.D. N M I

3 Aerial view of portion of the Hill of Tara, Co. Meath, the seat of the high kings of Ireland. The view shows in the foreground two ring-forts (dwelling-sites), the Forradh and 'Cormac's House'. In the top left-hand corner the Rath of the Synods, occupied from the second to the fourth century A.D., may be seen, and just below it a mound known as 'the Mound of the Hostages'—actually a Bronze Age burial site

4 Fragments of Roman silver from Balline, Co. Limerick. From a hoard of c. A.D. 400—loot brought back from an Irish raid on Roman Britain. N M I

5 A dress-fastening of the type known as a 'latchet', of enamelled bronze. Overall length 6½ in. c. sixth century A.D. N M I

6 The early monastery of *Sceilg Mhichil*, off the coast of Kerry, viewed from the peak of the Great Skellig Rock. The cluster of beehive cells may be seen over the cliffs in the centre foreground

7   The crudely shaped cross-slab, carved on the face with a Latin cross in low relief, which stands in the centre of the main enclosure of the monastery of *Sceilg Mhichíl*. Height 7 ft. Seventh century A.D.

8   The largest of the monastic cells on Skellig, built in corbelled, dry-stone technique. A simple Greek cross, picked out in pieces of quartz, may be seen just above the small opening near the crown of the cell

9   Church on St MacDara's Island, Co. Galway. The influence of timber construction is shown in the projecting *antae* and barges on the gable end

10 Aerial view of monastery on Inishcaltra (Holy Island), Lough Derg, Co. Clare. A scatter of monastic buildings, a Round Tower and traces of enclosures may be seen

11 Boat-shaped oratory at Gallarus on the Dingle peninsula, Co. Kerry. Here the corbelling technique of the beehive cells is adapted to a rectangular structure, and a thin mortar is used in the core of the masonry

12 General view of part of the monastic site at Glendalough, Co. Wicklow, showing Round Tower, St Kevin's Church (in foreground), the Cathedral (to the right of the Round Tower) and remains of a small church in right foreground. These buildings are all of about the tenth century A.D.

13 Grave-slab with incised ornamental cross and inscription in Irish: O̅R̅ DO AIGIDIU ('A Prayer for Aigidiu'). At Durrow, Co. Offaly

14 Grave-slab with inscription in *ogam* and majuscule script in Irish: COLMAN BOCHT ('Colman the Poor'). At Clonmacnoise, Co. Offaly

15 Aerial view of a single-banked ring-fort at Cashel, near Dungiven, Co. Derry. Many thousands of these earthworks, of which this is a typical example, marking habitation sites of the Early Christian period, still remain in Ireland

16 Aerial view showing in foreground Crannog No. 83, Ross Townland, Lough Gara, Co. Sligo. Many lake-dwellings like this were inhabited in Early Christian Ireland, but the type is known from much earlier, prehistoric times in the country

17 Tiny gold brooch or badge in the form of a bird, with spiral ornament in gold beaded filigree, from ring-fort at Garryduff, Co. Cork. This may be an import. Greatest length ½ in. Cork Public Museum

18 Detail of initial from the manuscript known as the *Cathach* of St Columba. The Capitals are embellished in red and yellow. Late sixth century A.D. Royal Irish Academy Library, Dublin

19 Head of the Tara brooch, front. Of gilt-bronze, with ornament of gold filigree, amber, enamel and amethyst settings. Diameter of ring 3½ in. *c.* A.D. 700. N M I

20 Detail of the Moylough belt-shrine, showing the buckle counter-plate

21 Front portion of cast-bronze shrine for leather belt, from a bog at Moy-lough, Co. Sligo. The decorative panels have embossed silver spirals, L-shaped cells of red and yellow enamel, squares of millefiori glass and studs of dark blue paste with silver insets. Eighth century A.D. N M I

22 The Ardagh Chalice: of silver with ornamental panels and handles with gold filigree, coloured enamels and gilt-bronze cast ornament. Found in a hoard with other objects, some of slightly later date, at Ardagh, Co. Limerick. Height 7 in. Early eighth century A.D. N M I

23 Detail of chip-carved bronze gilt decoration on stem of Ardagh Chalice

24 Detail of the Tara brooch showing filigree interlacing, spirals and animal patterns

25 Detail of decorative band below the rim of the Ardagh Chalice, showing ring-punching and animal interlacing in gold filigree

26 Animal pattern in gold filigree from handle, Ardagh Chalice

27 Medallion and portion of border of the Ardagh Chalice, showing glass and enamel studs, filigree ornament, and portion of the inscription showing in reserve bronze against a punched background

28 Cast-bronze plaque of Crucifixion, possibly from a book-cover. The group includes the lance- and sponge-bearers and two angels, with ornamental spirals, fret-patterns and interlacing. From Athlone, Co. Westmeath. Height approx. 8 in. Eighth century A.D. N M I

29 House-shaped reliquary from Lough Erne. Box of yew-wood with cast-bronze plates and ornamental attachments. This, with its hipped roof and ridge-pole with decorated finials, seems to have been a common type of early shrine and several Irish and Scottish examples are known. Height approx. 6 in. Eighth century A.D. N M I

30 Cast-bronze crest of a bell-shrine from Killua Castle Collection, showing stylized human figure between two fantastic animals. This motif, which is common in Early Christian art both in Ireland and on the Continent, derives ultimately from the East. Breadth 5 in. Eighth century A.D. N M I

31 Detail of face from Killua Castle bell-shrine. The treatment of the features and hair strikingly recalls the conventions of La Tène art

32 Figure of St Matthew from Collectanea MS. 1395, St Gall, Switzerland. St Matthew is here depicted as a scribe and is dipping his pen or brush into an ink-horn fixed to his chair. Eighth century A.D. Cathedral Library, St Gall

33 Figure of St Mark from St Gall Gospel-book 51. The symbols of the Four Evangelists occupy the corners of the page. Cathedral Library, St Gall

34 Beginning of Genealogy of Christ, folio 200R, Book of Kells. *c.* A.D. 800. Trinity College Library, Dublin

35 Virgin and Child, folio 7V, Book of Kells. Depictions of the Virgin and Child are rare in Irish art, but representations similar to this occur on Early Christian ivories from Egypt and Gaul, and on High Crosses on Iona and Islay, Scotland

36 South Cross at Ahenny, Co. Tipperary. The spiral and interlacing styles of the metalwork appear here in carved sandstone, and the five bosses of the cross-head seem to imitate metal rivet-heads. Height approx. 11 ft. Eighth century A.D.

37 North Cross at Ahenny. The scene visible on the base in this view is similar to carvings on some Pictish monuments in Scotland. Height approx. 12 ft. Eighth century A.D.

38 Spiral ornament from the North Cross at Ahenny. The spirals at the four corners terminate in triplets of bird-heads with gaping beaks; the whole pattern is closely related to patterns in metalwork

39 Front of the brooch from Killamery, Co. Kilkenny. In form closely related to the penannular brooches, but with three links joining the expanded terminals. Diameter over 4 in. *c.* A.D. 850. N M I

40 Large brooch from Ardagh, Co. Limerick. Diameter about 6 in. Ninth century A.D., with the chip-carved ornament characteristic of the period. N M I

41 Detail of back of Killamery brooch, showing panels with animals

42 Brooch from Fossensviet, Fossen, Nord-Trondelag, Norway. This and the other objects on the same page are examples of the many objects brought back to Scandinavia as Viking loot and found in Viking graves in Norway. Trondheim Museum

43 Irish mounting, with animal ornament, from a man's grave of *c.* A.D. 900. N. Kaupang, Vestfold, Norway. Universitetets Oldsaksamling, Oslo

44 Irish mounting from a woman's grave of the ninth century. N. Kaupang, Vestfold, Norway. Universitetets Oldsaksamling, Oslo

45 Irish mounting from a woman's grave of the ninth century. Bjaland, Telemark, Norway. Universitetets Oldsaksamling, Oslo

46 Viking sword from Ballinderry, Co. Westmeath. The vine-patterned guard bears the name Hiltepreht, and the blade the name Ulfberht. Length 36½ in. Ninth century A.D. N M I

47 Hilt of a Viking sword from Islandbridge cemetery, Dublin, with ornament of metal inlays on guard and pommel. Ninth century A.D. N M I

48 Silver penannular brooch of 'Hiberno-Viking' type, with animal ornament. Find-place unknown. Diameter of ring 5 in. *c.* A.D. 900. N M I

49 Head of kite-shaped brooch with crude animal figures ornamented with granulation, possibly from Clonmacnoise. Height of head, 2¼ in. *c.* A.D. 1000. N M I

50 Head of thistle brooch of silver from Ardagh, Co. Limerick. Diameter of ring 3 in. N M I

51 Panel depicting the Flight into Egypt, from the High Cross at Moone, Co. Kildare. The theme is common in the sculpture of the High Crosses but the style of the figure-carving here is confined to the granite crosses of the Barrow valley

52 Panel depicting Daniel in the Lions' Den from the Cross of Moone. This is one of the commonest themes of the High Cross carvings, and is common also outside Ireland, e.g. on Burgundian belt-buckles

53 Combat of lions and serpents from the Cross at Moone. The carving here is very like Pictish stone-sculpture in Scotland

54 Shaft of a cross at Clonmacnoise, showing a horseman and three lions in low relief. Here again there is a strong resemblance to some Pictish work

55 Cross of Patrick and Columba, Kells, Co. Meath. Height 13 ft. Ninth century A.D.

56 Head of Muiredach's Cross, Monasterboice, Co. Louth, with depiction of the Crucifixion at the crossing. This is the finest example of a Scripture Cross. Early tenth century A.D.

57 Panel showing the Arrest of Christ, from Muiredach's Cross. This panel provides an excellent illustration of the costume, weapons and ornaments of the period

58 Crook of the Kells Crosier, showing the ornithomorphic openwork crest. Greatest breadth approx. $7\frac{1}{2}$ in. Tenth century A.D. The collar-knop, with its foliate pattern, is an addition of the eleventh century. British Museum

59 Knop 1 of the Kells Crosier. Height $3\frac{1}{2}$ in.

60 Knop 3 of the Kells Crosier. Height $3\frac{1}{2}$ in.

61 Middle knop of St Dympna's Crosier. Tenth century A.D. Height $2\frac{3}{8}$ in. N M I

62 Figure in cast bronze of a bishop with crosier, from the drop of St Mel's Crosier. Height $2\frac{3}{4}$ in. St Mel's College, Longford

63 The Rock of Cashel, Co. Tipperary, the seat of the kings of Munster and later of the Archbishops of Cashel. The Round Tower is probably of the eleventh century; the other buildings are of the later medieval period

64 Panel from St Molaise's book-shrine showing an ecclesiastic holding a book, against a background of interlaced animals. Height approx. 3 in. Early eleventh century A.D. N M I

65 Crest of St Patrick's bell-shrine, with cast-bronze openwork ornament of Urnes character. The motif of the main panel—a vine with birds— is very ancient and widespread in Christian art but is comparatively rare in Ireland. Breadth $4\frac{1}{2}$ in. *c*. A.D. 1100. N M I

66 Detail from the shrine of the *Breac Maodhóg*. Eleventh century A.D. N M I

67 Detail of crook of the Crosier of the Abbots of Clonmacnoise, showing inlaid animal pattern of Ringerike-Urnes style. The details of the animal head here (top, centre) are those of the carvings on Urnes church in Norway. Late eleventh century A.D. N M I

68 Cross of Cong, shaft. Made for Toirdelbach Ua Conchubhair, king of Connacht, in *c.* A.D. 1123 to enshrine a relic of the True Cross. The bronze openwork animal patterns are one of the finest examples of the Irish Urnes style. N M I

69 Cross of Cong, ornamental knop and animal head

70 Cormac's Chapel, Cashel, south façade. Built by Cormac Mac Car-thaigh, king of Munster, in A.D. 1127–34

71 The 'Doorty' Cross at Kilfenora, Co. Clare, with carvings of ecclesiastics carrying three different types of crosier. Twelfth century A.D.

72 Cross at Dysert O Dea, Co. Clare, with carvings depicting the Cruci-fixion and a bishop. The base bears an interlace of serpents in the Urnes style. Height 12 ft. 8 in. Twelfth century A.D.

73 Doorway at Killeshin, Co. Laois. Built by Diarmait Mac Murchada, king of Leinster, *c.* A.D. 1160

74 Detail from intrados of arch of Romanesque doorway at Killeshin, showing low-relief carving of chevrons with pellets, foliage and animals

75 Portion of arch of Romanesque doorway at Dysert O Dea, Co. Clare, showing human heads and chevrons. Twelfth century A.D.

76 The Nuns' Church at Clonmacnoise, with carved Romanesque doorway and chancel arch. *c.* A.D. 1166

Index

Early Christian Ireland